T0167228

Life on Life's Terms
"My Gratitude Speaks"

Frankie Marie

iUniverse, Inc.
Bloomington

Life on Life's Terms "My Gratitude Speaks"

iUniverse books may be ordered through booksellers or by contacting:

iUniverse
1663 Liberty Drive
Bloomington, IN 47403
www.iuniverse.com
1-800-Authors (1-800-288-4677)

ISBN: 978-1-4697-0908-6 (sc)
ISBN: 978-1-4697-0910-9 (hc)
ISBN: 978-1-4697-0909-3 (e)

Printed in the United States of America

iUniverse rev. date: 12/22/2011

Special Thanks

I dedicate this book to my sponsor for giving me the courage to never give up and let my imagination go wild, for always being strong and never being ashamed for who I am, who I was or who I have become as a woman from all my experiences and paths life has given me. For loving me unconditionally and never judging me for all my wrongs and rights, for being the friend of my life, for always giving me the look in my eyes with confidence, trust. She has given me many gifts…unconditional love, faith to believe all is wrapped in a dream…for within this dream is laughter and passion, excitement, trust and consuming need. Thank you Debbie for being my rock.

To Carrie S my friend from Texarkana AR who has unconditionally stood by our friendship regardless the trials and tribulations that are put in front of us, you never give up on me no matter what, you are kind, loving and the most trusting person I have ever met, Thank you my sweet Carrie.

To Roni and Eddie Dyas from Fouke AR, they have not only become my friends engraved in my heart but my Family that I will treasure forever, they have walked me through good and bad times and have been there for me unconditionally, they have taught me to never forget my strength and my values, they gave me hope where hope was gone. I love you guys.

To Tanya Rosa from California and my sponsor's Jan may she "rip" and Debbie my sponsor I have now, I love you all so much.

To my children for understanding me and always knowing that no matter what, I was there mother and giving me that unconditional love, strength and courage that I can conquer anything. My oldest son, My Daughter and my youngest son I love you kids with every breath I take. And Kristy my step daughter who always loved me unconditionally with no reservations no matter what, she never gave up on me and was there anytime I needed, Thank you Kristy for your strength and courage you always gave me. I love you so much.

To my Mother the greatest one of all whom I cherish with all my heart and love unconditionally and my Father for understanding my feelings and supporting my choices once I got my life back, and once he started his. To my siblings that found faith in me and encouraged me, you know who you are; I adore you with all my heart. To my Best Friend Gary for always reminding me where I came from and where I was at that moment, I am grateful to you. For taking on responsibilities with my son and showing him what love and family values really are, even though he wasn't your blood you showed no difference and took him in your heart. And most of all my support group's from Santa Cruz California and Texarkana Texas/Arkansas.

This journey has truth, imagination, fiction and people who don't exist as well as do exist to help you understand and Make it in life on life's terms. May God be with you and bless you, May you carry hope within your heart to never give up, I hope with my Book I will give you the courage to always have faith and never give up.

Not now but in the coming years we will come to know the meaning of our tears and someday we will understand. So Enjoy today to the fullest, because tomorrow is not promised.

One morning you may never wake up; tell all your friends you love them! I was thinking…I could die today, tomorrow or next week, and I wondered if I had any wounds needing to be healed, friendships that needed rekindling or three words needing to be said. Let every one of your friends and family knows you love them. Even if you think they don't love you back, you would be amazed at what those three little words and a smile can do. And just in case GOD calls me home before I see you again "I love you"

It hasn't been easy, but from my heart, and soul, smiles, tears and prayers along with my experiences strengths and hopes. My goal is to give you hope and inspire you to never give up with "Life on life's terms".

Frankie Marie

The Cries Within

I can remember how my parents espoused the "what will people think" philosophy, in public we really did pull off the "perfect Family" image, we were all very gracious to each other, at home mom and dad changed from smiling, chatting and joking to dad completely withdrawing with his beers and mom yelling for attention. Its like I always had a feeling of "preparing for" or getting ready for something and my brother who was just under me felt the same way, we both thought a lot alike, all we had at that time was each other and we always knew what one or the other was thinking. I had a role, always a flurry of household chores to get right and my smaller brother and sisters to take care of but I felt happiest in the midst of my chores, I learned early on how to bottle up my feelings because they didn't matter anyways so why even try to express them. I consciously worked at not needing anything from anyone again to hopefully cut down on some of the stress, if they even cared. That's how I felt, my words didn't matter at that time and keeping my mouth shut was the best thing I could do for all of us to avoid an argument or getting hit and being told that what I said didn't matter or was stupid. So I learned to bottle up tensions by anticipating what needed to be done next to make it at least easier for mom and the kids, wasn't there fault the life we were in at that time sucked. But then again they had no idea of the abuse that was going on in that house and I was at fault also to hide it from them every time I had a chance, I felt they didn't need to know what was going on or have to live in any kind of fear, that was my job and mine only, even though Pat always wanted to be a part of and seemed like he just had to protect me I felt he just wasn't old enough to know everything, so I let him go with only what he saw and heard, the rest I kept to myself, it was bad enough I didn't need to share it with anyone.

Being raised in child abuse, physical, sexual or mental is very common in the world I lived in, doesn't mean it was ok but we didn't have places to reach out back then like we have today.

Child abuse is common in all sorts of troubled families. While severe physical abuse and overt sexual abuse are clearly recognizable as traumatic to infants and children, other forms of child abuse may be more difficult to recognize as being abusive, meaning getting into the adults, your scared for life and the only one that can help you is YOU, in having the will to overcome the trauma.

I'm 54 years old today and it's only been a few years that I had finally let go of all the secrets and overcome the trauma I kept deep inside my soul, I didn't want know one to know because of what they would think of me or how I would be treated because of it, or what would it do today to the family that had hurt me considering that they were different people today, sober and better parents, I was willing to simply keep that secret till I died so that know one would be hurt by the actions that had been put on me all those years ago, was it worth having them relive that pain, or even cause a huge fight within that family because of what was done all those years ago? I wasn't out to hurt anyone at all, I have been clean from drugs for 14 years now and hearing all these stories from people who shared there experiences, strengths and hopes at the meetings of Narcotics Anonymous that I went too kept digging inside of me, I felt like I was a fraud not telling about all that had happened to me, I would glorify my story a little to avoid telling about the shameful things I carried deep in my heart, I didn't want people to judge me and I wanted them to think I was not one of them, I didn't do drugs because I was abused for so many years but it did play a role into the feelings I had at the time, the no self worth, the pain, the worthlessness I thought I was no matter how much I tried or did good it hunted me, at the end of a great day and I would sit at home to finally resting there it popped up in my head as if it was talking to me saying, "why don't you just let me out" "are you afraid of hurting the ones who did this to you" or "are you living a lie to feel better then others" I would close my eyes wishing it would just go away but it never did, thanks to the help of my wonderful sponsor Debbie here in Texarkana and my best friend Carrie that would always tell me how good I was as a person, how I could make a difference in peoples lives because of all I had been through and how they knew for a fact that I could help change another's life forever by simply sharing my story. It killed me so I decided to write my first book and just let it out, as much as I at the time could remember and to my surprise as I would finish one secret and began to tell o another I would feel better and better, like if I was taking this power away from anyone who had hurt me, even though at the time they were alcoholic or what the problem was, and even though today they had been sober for years and doing great and treating you as if you were so special and liking having someone love you that much it was like I didn't care no more, yes I cared about there feelings today very much so, but I needed to get this out of me, it's been long over due and I needed peace with myself, I needed to get rid of the secrets knowing that there are so may other out there like me that needed to know how or what to do to get rid of these painful secrets, I felt like I had been the one chosen to reach out and help, what really did it for me was I had went to a women's facility to speck and tell my story of what I did in the past with drugs and what I did to be who I am today, there stares were like infatuated and so interested in what did they have to do to be different and get away from drugs, my job was to guide them in the right direction with my story. After I had spoke they stood up and gave a applaud with smiles that wet from ear to ear, I was I shock to see how much they looked up to me and after the meeting they were full of questions and kept saying to me, "when I get out of here I'm going to do like you did so I can have my life back." a sharp pain hit my heart, I knew a lot of them had been abused and a lot of them ended up there because of it, they knew nothing else but the abuse so it lead them to drugs so that they would no longer feel no pain, the drugs made you feel like know one will ever again hurt you, you felt like you were the strongest person alive and most of all, you weren't afraid anymore. When I left that facility that evening I told myself I needed to get honest with myself ad be ok wit sharing about me being abused for 11 years, not that it lead me to drugs but it gave me a sense of no self worth and always doing things so people would like me because I didn't know how to be strong o my own, it lead me to allow people to abuse me in other ways because I didn't know how to defend my self or say "no" and I did so many things I my life just to please people because I wanted them to like me or accept me, even in my years of being clean I still did it. As I drove home that evening I thought of all that stuff and decided it was time to let go of all the secrets, it was time to take away the power from anyone who thought they got away with it or the power of simply letting me agree with them even if I didn't want too ad they knew it. I was done, that was it, as of tonight I was going to finish my book and let it all out, no more secrets no more lies and it was time for me to live my life pain free from then till now. I knew as I started to write that night that there would be people I my family that would be very upset that I would do this but I wasn't doing it to hurt anyone, I was doing it to free myself, it wasn't about them anyways it was about me and I knew that if I was totally honest that there was a lot of others out there that simply needed to know it was ok and what to do to get out of that rut no matter how old you are. I had made up my mind and I was going to do it, I would take away the power from anyone who thought they would change my mind or who felt they could still manipulate me, it wasn't going to work, this was for "me to make a difference in someone else's life" my goal was to be able to help someone like me out there and hope they can move on and live there life free and clear from any kind of pain or secret that's holding them back.

My Gratitude speaks

It's July 4th 2007, 5 in the morning The smell of coffee roaming threw the house , my body hurts, I'm tired but the only thought in my mind is Today I have 12 years clean, I'm married to a man sent from heaven, he's a gift I still wonder why me!! He is the most wonderful man I have ever met. I am working doing what I love best, I work in recovery and my goal is "to make a difference". I'm a grandma to 3 lovely wonderful little girls that put's a smile on my face every time I see them…and can't wait for my oldest son to give me yet another grandchild… I get a flash of the past that runs threw my head, just so I never forget where I came from and what I have been threw. To think I have gone from, abuse, which is sexual to verbal to mental, with drugs, jails and institutions, from hitting bottom and climbing back up. From self destruction to rehabilitation and living life on life's terms.

Know that priorities come into play a lot in this book, as well as choices, how do you make right or wrong choices or how do you know when priorities come into play, and to always remember, it's not about the pain inflicted on you but what you do about it. Even though the past did not prepare me for what I was about to face threw this journey, It has taught me exactly where my priorities lie and what choices I feel the need to make on a daily bases.

Even though "Our priorities are quite strange," "We're missing a lot of opportunities (to do) a lot of good that America used to do and has a history of doing". My series of calculations didn't quite hit the spot with my self worth.

Remembering back 5 years ago when I worked for the courts I would see people's faces glisten with sweat, their red-rimmed eyes stare ahead vacantly as they're herded into the sweltering room where another day of court is about to begin.

Most of the men here have been arrested on drug charges; most of the women — some barefoot, some in stiletto heels — have been accused of prostitution. Few can afford lawyers.

Everybody else is represented by the same public defender, which hasn't had time to interview anyone beforehand. It's the commissioner in blue jeans peeking out from under her black robe that flips through manila folders and questions the prosecutor. My mind was ready to take on the day to give my best performance in defending first time drug offenders trying to give them the benefit of doubt and try to feel how it felt when at one time I was in there shoes hoping for that second chance. Wasn't easy because when you have know one to believe you and you're backed in your own corner your lost and have no hope.

The biggest surprise for me on turning 50 is how much it feels like being in junior high again. Suddenly, the women in my world are spending hours in front of the bathroom mirror, fiddling with their hair and micro-examining their complexions. They fret over their bodies in ways not seen since eighth grade. And even highly intellectual friends, who used to think nothing of showing up at conferences in drip-dry suits, have begun to give to fashion magazines the same scrutiny they give research papers. At parties or even at the playground, I'm aware of the x-ray stares checking out my outfit, my shoes, my hair, followed by the silent registration of approval — or disapproval. Women always do this to each other, of course, but at 52 you're aware of heightened inspection: "Hmm, she's looking older. Is her hair lighter? She looks much 'rested' — maybe she got her eyes done?"

Its like friendships they come and they go, are they really worthy of your trust or hard work in spending your time giving them that unconditional friend that you are. You will see threw out my book that friendships come and go and very little can you actually say "she or he is my best friend",

I can count on one hand what a true friend really is, and to be honest that's way to many, but enough to always know someone does care to that extent and you can actually count on them to be there for you unconditionally.

Whatever you do don't try to rekindle your friendship if your heart isn't into it, forcing yourself would make it fake. Most friendships end, and yours did when a confession of feelings was made in a negative way. Are you still friends with your best friend from kindergarten? College? First job? Friendships last while both parties are in a similar stage in life and then more often than not, dissolve. If you attempt a friendship with this man or woman, he or she will think you got back in touch because he or she has a chance with you. Leave well enough alone, guard your marriage and let your friend move on with his or her life. If you truly care for him or her, you will allow them to get over you and not have you remind them that they can't have you by hanging around him or her.

These are just few statements that you will experience threw out my book and to better make you understand me, I'm putting you at easy to begin with knowing my thinking today has extremely changed between then and now and living life on life's terms, with myself and with GOD.

When I was little and Not understanding life on life's terms and the concept of having to depend on the adults around me I was a very lost soul, the child with no clue of what was about to happen in her life.

The Innocence

I can remember as far back as when I was five years old, we lived in a small suburb in Paris France where there was a small house and woods near the back yard, I was always afraid to go near those woods thinking there was awful monsters there, considering I was always afraid of spiders and snakes or any kind of bug or moving creature. I was playing in the front yard with my little brother putting rocks in a American coffee can then making a wee sound as we threw them over our heads, and hearing our mother coming out yelling at us to stop throwing the rocks. After a few times of doing this my mother had come out and took the coffee can away from us and threw it in the air thinking it would not be near us to use again, as she said "stop playing with the gravel" and she walked away, but all the sudden I feel a THUMP on my head followed by red blood running down my face, the can she threw had come right down on my head and cutting it pretty bad. At the time my mother was getting ready to wash diapers and had filled the sink with Clorox and water, she heard me and came out to see why the heck I was crying for and she seen this red sheet of blood covering my face, her first reaction was to grab me and run me in the house and put the top of my head right in that Clorox and water, talk about pain, till this day I will never forget it, god that hurt so bad, my soon to be step dad and my mother rushed me to the hospital where I received 24 stitches. I learned from then on to NOT throw the rocks in the driveway. The next day I was out in the back yard and I remember sitting there for hours looking at those woods back there, I was so scared of them, thinking there was some kind of monster because of the echo's the wind made going threw there was to frightening to me. My brother who was smaller then I was by a few years wanted to go look in those woods as well as this kid called Alan adopted by my grandfather who was about the same age as I was. He insisted on wanting to go in those woods just to look, I was so scared and decided to follow him just a little ways, as we entered the hallow woods with thick tree's and so dark even during the day, my heart was beating one hundred miles a hour I was so afraid. We barely would make it to the entrance and some little noise would scare us to death and we would run out screaming as if we were being chased by the monsters. My step father "who was always drunk" was so upset at me for crying about it that I wet my pants, he would take me out back to this shed and make me bend over a sawhorse and whoop me with a thin twig over and over until I begged him to stop. I used to hate him for that, he got pleasure in doing that, then he would come and hug you after he had a few beers and expected to make it all better. There were times when my step dad wasn't there and mom would spend time with me or try, I know she had her things she did but I knew she loved me and I really think she felt sorry for me at times. She was so pretty, I would sit for ever just watching her wishing that one day I look like her. Her smile would lighten up a room, her hair was so soft and she would let me brush it when she was in the mood, I loved her so much. I wanted her attention so bad that I did things that only got me in trouble and didn't really know it.

I also sucked my thumb and I would get woke up out of a dead sleep yelling because my step father would bite my thumb so hard, he would put hot mustard on it when I slept or one time he put hot wax on it, I remember crying for days, but I just wouldn't stop sucking my thumb, it was to me my only security I guess. He was drunk every time he did this so to him it wasn't a big deal; he hardly remembered it the next day. To me it was but I was so afraid of him and I didn't know I was even doing it because during the day I never sucked my thumb out of fear but in my sleep I did.

My step dad was in the army and he was a American solider so he was gone a lot and trust me I didn't miss him at all with his beer drinking watching him hit mom and then of course me. But I liked the other men that came to the house they were American but always so nice to me, brought me little toys and gave me hugs every time they seen me, I thought all men were nice until my step dad came home because it wasn't at all the same when the other Americans were there.

One day as I sat out side I was picking flowers and I see a tall man walk in the driveway and he waves to me with a bright smile, I waved back with a shy look, he got closer to me and knelt to his knee as he said to me, come here little one and as I did he hands me a rag doll and he touched my long hair as he whispered to me you are so beautiful my child, then he caressed my cheek, all I did was smile back at him and couldn't help looking at his eyes he had big brown eyes with long eye lashes that's what had intrigued me and his smile was white as white can be. But it didn't last long I hear the door open and my mother grabs me away from him and yells at him to never again come near me she then took the doll back and threw it at him telling him to leave, as he did he looked at me and winked as he says "next time we meet will be for good little one" and he walked away, my mother jerked me in the house and I had to stay in the laundry room until her friend that was there left and then she made me go to the bedroom where I had to sit there till dinner or till my step dad got home and she said I was going to get whooped again for excepting that doll from a stranger.

Not long after that we had moved to the south of France called Normandy where there were more Americans then I ever seen in my life we stayed at my mother's friends place which was a hotel and the friend was a man with like 8 kids and 2 wife's. IT was strange but I was too small to ever try to figure that out and what that was all about. All I know is we would play with all the kids and have so much fun out side with the American men because they would play games with us and built swings for us and gave us American canned food and candy. I was happy there when we first got there because I wasn't getting whooped no more and I had kids to play with that were my age and younger. I had a little brother but he was too small to play with. Come night time after us kids were fed we were put to bed up stairs and the noise began from downstairs, we could hear them all having fun, partying and laughing loud so me and my little friend Rob and frank who was my age would sneak to the edge of the stairs and watch as we looked down to see what they were all doing, to my surprise they were having more fun then we thought, I remember me and Rob giggling as we watched the American men at the bar pulling women to there laps, kissing them, we would giggle so much not really knowing what they were doing. This would go on all the time every night we would be put to bed we would wait like 20 minutes then sneak to the stairs and watch threw the bars as they all partied and did silly things, I seen the women dance on the bar and men laughing and slapping the women on there butt's we would see them fight and do many weird things but it was entertaining to us and we loved watching all this until one day we got caught by one of the guys and they said something to our mothers, we ran to our room and hid under the sheets but it was too late we were busted. My step dad was drunk and he came up the stairs and grabbed me by the arm and jerked me out of bed almost dragging me to the top of the stairs and I could hear my mother screaming at him to let me go but he was so mad about something else that this didn't help, he held me to the top of the stairs threatening to my mother he was going to drop me down and she was so upset that Frank's mother grabs a thick glass ashtray and threw it at him hitting him in the head so hard it knocked him out but mean while as he fell I went down too and rolled down the stairs, I remember the Americans and my mother grabbing me to see if I was ok and where I was hurt and there laid my step dad with a bloody head and passed out. When all was finally over with I was put back to bed and the door was shut so I couldn't hear what else had happened, I had fallen asleep.

The next few weeks were the same. Parties at night and work during the day, Robert and frank's mother's we called them aunt even though they wasn't related to us. They had taken us for a walk out in the fields where there were cows and goats, Frank, Rob and I would always stay together we was best friends and we were close to each other for little kids, all we had was each other to play with or anything it was always them and me. The Americans would give us rides in there jeeps and give us all kinds of American things from food to toys, we liked them they were all so nice to us kids. But the fun didn't last, we were going to be moving to America with my step dad so I would probably never see Rob again, Frank and his parents were moving to America also I remember my mother telling me we had a week to pack then we was going on a big plane to America, she was pregnant, there was me and my little brother, and the big day came, we said our goodbyes and I remember looking back at my friend Robert as we drove away in a American bus like truck, I waved as I watched him get farther n farther away.

Going To America

The plane ride was so long I was the kind of kid that couldn't sit still so it was so hard for me to sit for hours on end, I was six years old and got so sick on that plane, I couldn't eat I kept throwing up, I tried to drink but it wasn't staying down, then one of the hosts asked to take me up stairs, we were on a bowing 747 where the lady took me up stairs and sat me near the bar where there was cool air and she gave me 7-up to drink and I started to feel better, I as well was loving the attention I was getting, my mom would give me lots of attention but when my step dad was there she couldn't and I understood for some reason, I think it was the look in her eyes she would give me. It was that I'm sorry look. We finally got to our destination, Oregon where my step dad's parents lived and where our new home was going to be. I remember meeting my new grandmother and grandfather, they were so nice, my new grandma was especially nice to me for some reason and I loved it. She taught me so much threw out the years, taught me how to do things for myself and not expect someone to do it for me.

Life in America seemed different to me, maybe because everyone spoke a language I didn't understand, being put in a school where I didn't understand a word they said, spending my days alone in the backyard or in the house. As time went on I had learned the American language and made friends as well as living life the American way, so I thought. My step Father was an alcoholic and it seemed necessary for him to abuse me as a child, he would get drunk find a reason to get mad at me. I was scared and just a little girl but I knew it wasn't right; I did as I was told because I was so afraid of him.

I sucked my thumb at 6 years old and in the middle of the night he would come in and bite my thumb so hard I would wake up out of a dead sleep screaming, or he felt hitting me with the belt across the legs and back was necessary to diseplene me. But then he would get all nice and make me do things saying I won't be in trouble no more. I had a younger brother at that time, he was so sweet and we were getting very close as we grew up, and my mother was expecting another baby. To watch my step father abuse my mother on a daily basis seemed to be normal to me, I thought it was a way of life because it's all I ever saw. I was young and didn't yet understand any concept of life and went with the flow as they call it in today's terms.

I am now 11 years old, 5 years later and nothing had changed, the abuse was there, watching mom get yelled at or hit just killed me so of course I would say something and he made sure I got my share of it too, I just wanted to die. I knew I Had a smart mouth towards him but I didn't care, when mom was home with me and she had that time with me I remember how she would tell me I was her best child. I loved hearing her say that. I now had 2 brothers and a sister and my mother was yet again expecting another baby, my step father was still a alcoholic even worse and the abuse in the house got worse, I would receive the beatings just like my mother, because if one of my brothers or sister did something wrong while on my watch when mom was working and I baby sat, I would take the blame just so they Would not have to suffer the pain I felt every time that belt came across my legs or back or getting thrown down on the floor or my head slapped against the wall until I would beg him to stop but by that time I would get so numb it didn't matter any more, all I knew is as long as it was me and not the kids that's all that mattered. My brother just under me started to see what was going on and he would start yelling at my step dad to leave me alone and he would take beatings at times just so I wouldn't get hit, I felt so bad but he would come to me and tell me that it was ok he was tired of seeing me get slapped around all the time. Him and I got very close and it seemed we took turns getting in trouble so the other kids wouldn't get hit, he was as well so brave and I loved him so much. He knew exactly what was going on and he felt so sorry for me but the only thing he could do was stand by me when it was time to get in trouble, the rest just killed him to know I was being abused and couldn't do nothing about it. But he knew it was either me or the girls so I rather take it so they would be left alone, all he knew to do is console me when it was over.

I missed a lot of school due to marks on me from every time I got hit, my grandmother was so nice though, I remember she would come over and just get so upset at her son once she seen me or my mother. I hurt, there were times I couldn't get out of bed but I had too so slowly I moved myself from room to room, I had to always make sure the house was always clean, dinner was done and do laundry all the time. My mother worked as a waitress where she had to wear these real short outfits and her top was very low cut she would work nights all the time and my step father worked as a driver for a big company, and sense I was the oldest it just seemed all the pressure was on me to make sure everything was done. My mother felt so bad and tried so much to make it up to me by doing things with me when we were alone but it wasn't easy for her either. I honestly don't think they realized how bad it really was, But Changing diapers, wiping snotty noses and entertaining the kids so they wouldn't get into things or do anything that would be a reason for yet another slap in the face or something thrown at you... And going to school acting like nothing ever happened at home and you acted like you had a normal life as a child.

I know my mom did her best to let me do some after school sports, we would have some time alone her and I when I did and I loved every minute of it, she had no idea how much I missed being with her I loved her so much, but seemed I never finished anything or was afraid to get too involved because I knew it wouldn't last.

I learned at a very young age the word "manipulation" meaning I knew exactly what to say and do to never give anyone the reason to question my burses or reasons why I had yet again missed school because I just didn't care. I would wish everyday to be 18 so I could run away and be free from this life, I watched TV. dreaming I could be like the women I seen in movies or soaps, seemed that dreaming was all I had at that time and that's the only thing that seemed to put a smile on my face back then.

I am now 16 years old and hated life, the abuse got worse then ever, the hitting got harder and the mental abuse did too. He still made the remarks and comments, this went on for years. I felt I had to protect my sisters and brothers and did anything I could to do so no matter what it was. The thought of killing myself had crossed my mind a few times, but my brother Pat knew my thoughts and would tell me to never think like that again, he was always there to protect me, even though he was younger then I was the only thing he knew to do to make me feel a little safer was to just be there for me when I needed someone to just hold me or talk to me and still he also took abuse just so I would get a break, we were like a team if you want to call it that, we would stand by each other always no matter what, if I did something wrong he would lie for me and if he did something wrong I would for him, all we had was each other and at that time it was a lot for us. I would skip school a lot because I didn't want to be around people that knew me from my town so I hung with kids from other schools and towns. I felt like life had no meaning, no purpose, that I was brought in this world to be the hated child and to be the built in babysitter and house keeper. My school work was failing badly and I didn't even care, I couldn't concentrate or focus, I wanted boys to like me and I wanted friends but that wasn't going to happen any time soon, being the way I was and looking the way I did didn't help either so I would try to be popular but ran with the wrong type of kids, the one's who skip out of school, the ones who drank and the ones who were just as bad off as I was if not worse, but I knew no difference yet so I didn't see there immaturities or there careless actions. I was about to have my sweet 16 Birthday party which was happening at a park, well it ended up being at a company picnic from my step dads work so I guess the fun was just as good as if I would have had a private party because I had no friends that would of even tried to come, my only real friend was my brother, I do remember mom got me a matching bedroom set, 2 beds with matching bedspreads, it was so awesome and she had gotten me new clothes, I could tell by her smile that she really was trying to make me happy and more then she knew she sure did. I was in high school and wanted to be a part of so bad but I just didn't fit in, I didn't have the right clothes or makeup or pretty jewelry like the popular girls had so I was always left out, a lot of the kids knew my mother worked for this restaurant where they wore short dresses and rumor had it that there was drugs and night life after closing hours, I didn't like what I would hear because despite all I loved my mother very much and was embarrassed when they would talk about her, It was bad enough they talked about my dad's drinking but didn't like it when it was about my mother. We lived in a very small town and everyone there knew you, about you and all you did if it was right or wrong everyone knew it. Everyone knew my dad was a alcoholic and mom was "easy to get along with" and to be honest I think she just wanted to be loved, or paid attention too, regardless her always being mad she had her times with me I would give anything to have time stand still when she was with me and paid me that small attention that she did, I know she loved me but I also know she was so confused and tired so if there was attention to get from a man she wouldn't pass it up and I didn't blame her.

I hated the nights my mom would work, I was afraid to be home with the kids alone with my step father, he was not only rude and mean, he didn't miss the opportunity to make mean comments to me every time I walked by him, I would sleep in my sisters room a lot or with my little brothers in fear he would come and be mean to them or me due to the comments he had made. I now had 2 sisters and 2 brothers, we had lost a brother due to health problems, my little baby brother was so cute, I loved him so much he was the one I took care of the most because he was so little even though I took care of all my brothers and sisters but he was like my special baby and he always wanted me, to feed him to put him down to play with to do anything it was always me he wanted so it felt good, my other brother who was just under me he was so sweet he and I always did things together we were each others best friends, he had character and was a outgoing little guy but he always stayed near me because he knew I was beig abused he just didn't know what to do about it as I didn't, but knowing he was there for me was all I needed at that time he was my best friend for years and as we grew older he would start taking the beatings just so I wouldn't because it killed him inside every time I would get yelled at or hit, we would tell each other everything and he would always say to me "if ever you leave please don't leave me here" and I would tell him I would always take him with me I loved him so much, he was my brother, my best friend, my everything. My sisters were daddy's little girls and hardly ever got in trouble it was always mine and my brother's fault if they did something wrong because my dad never would see there wrongs…I loved them though regardless how much they would get me and my brother in trouble. My sister J was so pretty, her smile was like a movie stars I remember always telling her she would be a movie star one day, her eyes were a blue that would make you melt she was simply a beautiful girl, my sister V who was a year younger then J was as well a pretty girl, she was so smart and very witty, she had that look in her innocent eyes that said "uh huh wait and see I will get my way" and she sure did but she was still my girl no matter what she did. They all were like my kids, I protected them like if they were my children, considering I was with them more then my parents were, I dressed them, bathed them, feed them, held them when they cried, put them to bed, played with them, whatever it took I was always there for them. Living in Co burg was a very ruff time for my parents, there relationship and being parents to us all, So that's where I stepped in and did my best to give these kids what I knew they wanted most, "mom and dad to be there". It just was possible at that time of there marriage that they had time for us kids when they were working all the time and trying to figure out what to do with each others lives, when they were home they would fight all the time or be mad at something I did or one of the kids, I would get yelled at for not doing good in school or not doing something with the kids that I was told to do and I had forgotten, I remember that my brother P had told me he was so sick and tired of them always yelling or mad about something that he wanted us to run away, we had just seen a movie on T V where the parents were gone and the kids took care of themselves and he had looked at me saying "we can do that" but I knew it was never possible and I carried so much fear within me I knew I could never do that. He knew I wasn't going to just pack these kids up and run away, so he just came and sat by me and we held each other and cried, we were so unhappy and sad know one even had a clue because we had learned at a young age to hide our feelings so we did. And we grew up doing that same thing, our lives ended up in shambles because of all the hurt we carried in our souls. I remember one time I had a friend spend the night which for me was like a dream come true because I never thought I would ever even have a friend that would take the time to want to be around me but this friend did, her name was D and she was about as homely as I was back in those days, we were in my room lights out just talking and I would hear the foot steps of my stepfather coming towards us as I did many nights, he never opened the door but would stand there for a while, I would shake in my blankets and pray he didn't come in. well this time we heard him, I had told D to lay still and pretend she is sleeping if he walked in my room, for the first time he did, I heard that knob turn and I about had a heart attack I started to shake and had tears running down wondering what was he going to do to us, the door slowly opened and we both lay there pretending we were asleep with our blankets wrapped around us so tight. He stood there for a few minutes and I could see threw a small hold in my blanket his image and not to my surprise he was so drunk, I gasped for air as in to hold my breath as tears ran down my cheek I thought for sure this was it and he was going to hurt us or me, at that time I felt so ashamed, hurt and scared, all these emotions build up just took me to a place of fear I had never felt before. I hear a noise as I peeked threw the hole and I watched him turn around and walk out, I let out a huge sigh but couldn't stop the tears from falling, thinking to myself why? Why did he do this and in front of my only friend in the world, what was she going to think or say now? Was my life really at an end this time? I didn't even know anymore, I lay there still and didn't move I was so ashamed, I heard D move from her bed but I still didn't take the covers away from my face I was too embarrassed to even face her, then I felt her hand move the covers from my face and she says to me, " its ok I know exactly how you feel and feel lucky that at least he walked out, at home mine doesn't walk out he comes in and locks the door"…my throat had a lump in it and I felt so bad now, I reached up and put my arms around her neck as we both cried together, that's when I knew I had a true friend and someone who really understood my fear and fears of life on life's terms. My brother P had heard me crying and snuck in my room all worried something had happened but when we told him what happened he was so relieved, he said he had heard the footsteps going to my room and he wanted so bad to just come out and tell him to get away but as I was he was afraid also, there was only so much he could do and to just be there for me where I didn't feel alone was more then he even knew.

D wasn't that great looking of girl back then or had anything going for herself, but she was the sweetest person you could know, she also had been around the block a few times so as far as relating to me, trust me when I say she could. We ended up being the best of friends as the years flew by and I had finally for the first time in my life found someone that would not only listen to me but as well understand me and it was the most precious thing in my life, to know there IS someone out there that is like you or is going threw the same fears or has gone threw the same feelings, and understood. That's when I realized what the word "grateful" meant and boy was I grateful and for the first time in my life I was actually happy that I wasn't judged.

I'm now 17 years old, not doing well in school at all, skipping out with other kids all because I wanted to be a part of, I thought I was popular if I did what they did or what they wanted, I had met them threw D or the back parking lot of the school, I never drank with them because just the smell of beer would make me sick from my step dad being a alcoholic , didn't smoke pot with them because I was to scared too and I didn't like the smell so I just hung out with them, and did the shoplifting stupid things teens sometimes do and yes D was right there with me my faithful friend, I wanted boys to like me because I wanted that male attention, I would kiss and make out with the boys but that was the extent of it, I would let them touch me on the back and legs but I never let them get any closer I was way to scared of that, even though my mother called me names a few times when I would sneak out of the house and she would finally find out or catch me, or show up at the school to take me to lunch just because and I wasn't there , it had become to where I didn't care what happened to me or what would be the consequence. I was at the point where I didn't like my mother for not protecting me from my step dad and I hated my step father for the way he treated me, and running away to me sounded great but I just couldn't leave the kids there without me or get the nerve enough to just go.

Still no friends except my friend D and I was ok with that, my parents still not doing to great and still fighting all the time, my step dad still drinking and things just don't look very good. I'm still doing the normal household stuff, helping out my mom. I felt it wasn't my responsibility but I did it anyways, maybe it's because I was older now and felt I had the experience to know what to do in raising a child due to the fact that I helped raise all the others. Even though I had D as my friend my brother P never let me get to far without him he was my buddy my best friend so I couldn't forget him, I had a bond with him, we were very close, he was getting older now he was just a couple years younger then I was and know one but I knew he was like me, "the bastard child" as my step father would call me when he was mad, he didn't even know to my knowledge that my brother wasn't even his, and if he did he hid it well. I was told by my aunt Janette that he wasn't my dads kid either and that P and I were bastard kids. But he as well would get the smacking around because he was older now and he would speak out if I would get hit, My step dad had made my mother give up a child when we lived in Colorado because it wasn't his, turned out to be a boy he was the 4th born child before my sisters and my little brother was born.

There were many times when he would yell at me I wanted to throw in his face how he made my mom give up a child how the second born wasn't even his but I never did because then it would hurt my mom and I didn't want that to happen, she was getting her share of beatings and abuse so I bit my tongue and never said a word about it and kept it for myself. I had over heard my mom talking to someone saying how my brother wasn't my step dads and to my surprise when we had spent some quality time just her and I together I had asked her and she told me. I believe with all my heart that my mom really tried to give me quality time with her when ever she could, I just didn't realize it at that time. My mother was finally tired of the abuse and drinking and had left a few times with us but she always went back after a few days, my dad would promise to stop drinking and she would believe him. They decided to have a long talk about what they needed to do to keep this family together.

My parents kept talking about moving back to France thinking it could be a better and fresh start for them from what I would over hear, I know they wanted to give it there best shot and here in America just wasn't working at this time, I as well was corresponding with a childhood friend Rob, we had been writing to each other for about 6 months.

Robs father was what you call The French Mafia Father. He did as he pleased when he wanted and how he wanted no matter what the consequence and he seemed to get away with anything. I would write to Robert in American because I had forgotten all my French, I would ask my mother to write for me but then again I didn't want her to know what I was writing to him for example how miserable I was at home, how I would get hit all the time or have to put up with a drunk dad while she was at work ect, so I would write in English and he would find a friend to translate my letters to him and when he wrote to me it was in French and my mother would translate for me until I got wise and started to ask the French teacher in school to translate for me and she also started to write them for me, so I sent him a lot more letters then my mother ever knew,

He sounded so nice, so strong, he had sent me a picture of him and its like I fell in love at first sight, the first man in my life that liked me for me, that felt some kind of sympathy for me and knew I wanted out of my situation real bad, he would make me feel so much better every time I got his letters he always added something that gave me courage, so when I over heard my parents talking about going back to France to give it another try at saving there marriage I would jump right in and encourage it as much as possible, I wanted to see Rob so bad and knew this would be my ticket to freedom if I just got there, I would tell my mother when we were alone that it's the best thing she could ever do and encourage anything I could, then when she was gone to work and dad was there I would do the same to him, I didn't care about there problems and if they solved them, all I cared about is getting to France to see Rob and hoped for a new life and future, he made promises to me in my letters that if I was with him it would be all different, he would take care of me, that we would get married and have children and that he loved me, that was the first time in my life a guy had said he loved me and didn't even have to sleep with me to tell me that or he hadn't even seen me except a picture and he loved me, I felt special, wanted and loved for the first time in my life and it felt so good I didn't want to let this feeling go.

A few months passed and I still wrote to Rob3 times a week if not more, I kept my normal routine as in caring for the kids when mom worked and cleaning as well as going to school when I could, times I just skipped out because I didn't want to be there, I wasn't popular and always made fun of, other times I couldn't be there because of burses left from the night before or day before due to getting slapped or kicked around either from my mom's rage towards me for something I didn't do right or my dads rage just because its what he did when he drank, plus my mouth didn't help I was always talking back and making the situation worse for myself.

My dad had a friend named Buddy who was also a drunk and he had this trailer that my dad let him park it in our yard and he stayed there for a few weeks. I hated him, he was a drunk, he would watch my every move and I was always scared of him, now did I not only have my dad to watch out for I had yet another drunk to watch out for, I wasn't stupid I seen the looks and the way they would brush against me passing in the hall or going threw a door, but I always acted dumb as if I didn't know what was going on and I was very careful to not give either one of them the idea I knew what they were doing or I knew I would be in big trouble once they were really drunk. I was doing dishes one night and I could feel something looking at me but I was the only one in the house with the kids my dad had stepped out to go see mom at the bar where she worked, it was dark out side but when I looked up I seen eyes looking right at me, I started to shake and didn't even look out the window I kept doing the dishes as fast as I could, I new it was buddy standing out there watching me. I hurried to finish then turned out the kitchen light and had the kids sit with me in the living room as we watched TV. I didn't care what we watched and I made sure it was something they wanted to watch so they would sit right there and not move. I would glance from the corner of my eye and I would still see him out there looking in. I was so afraid of him and wouldn't you know it that dad didn't come home that night either did mom, they had gotten into a fight and went there separate ways that night.

I remember it was late the kids fell asleep on the couch and so had I, when all the sudden I hear a pst pst sound and when I looked up there he stood, the drunk Buddy, he motioned for me to walk near him and I didn't move so he said to me come here or I will take your little sister. I started to have tears in my eyes thinking I will be damned if he even lays one hand on my sisters. I wanted to pinch my brother P so he knew but I couldn't reach him, so I walked towards him in the dark kitchen he started to try kissing on me, it was disgusting and I was scared but I pushed him back and went back towards my brothers and sisters. He just stood there looking at me and whispered that if I ever told my parents about him trying to kiss me that he would hurt me. So I never said a word in fear that my parents wouldn't believe me and would get so mad. But I did tell my brother P and he made sure bud was never near me alone again, It scared me to death every time I seen him and I would stay near my sisters and brothers so they were safe as well, I wouldn't leave there sight.

I was so happy one night I was in my room with the door closed and I could hear my parents talking, for the first time that I can remember my dad was sober and they even made sense. They had made up there minds to go to France. Oh my god I was so happy you have no idea, I was so thrilled I almost started to cry but instead I got on my knees and thanked GOD so much for answering my prayers and letting me finally see Rob again. That next day my mother told me about us all moving to France, I acted like I didn't know what they had talked about the night before and was excited and encouraged her until she was tired of hearing me talk about it. We had a huge garage sale sold everything we could think of, the focus those next few months was nothing but getting rid of everything we could and getting the hell out of here to go to France

The day finally came, my parents had the tickets for us all to leave and we were going to be leaving within the next few weeks, nothing made me happier and excited then to look forward to finally meeting Robert. Those weeks went by real fast and before I knew it we were on the plane going to France. We arrived at the airport in France, it was a very long flight and I had shoe's on that were a half size to small so my feet were killing me but I was used to pain so I didn't even care, all I remember is when coming off the plane I could hardly walk my feet hurt so bad and there he stood, the love of my life, oh he was so handsome and tall, with his big brown eyes and blonde hair, he didn't even look French he looked like a American but I didn't care he was beautiful to me and when our eyes met it was like love at first sight, he walked towards us and shook my dad's hand, gave my mom a hug and then he looked right in my eyes and gave me a hug, I could feel him shaking so bad as I was also, I couldn't take my eyes off him he was so handsome, he was there with his mother and father but I didn't even pay attention to all of them all I saw was Rob and it felt so good.

On the trip from the airport to there house was like a 4 hour drive so

Rob sat in the back seat with me and my sisters and my parents were in the front, my brothers were in another car with Rob's parents. His leg was touching mine sense we were pretty squeezed in that back seat and out of the blue he reached over and grabbed my hand in his but kept it hidden on the seat between our legs touching, I remember he just couldn't keep his eyes off me and I felt so special, so wanted and I didn't want that feeling to end, I was 17 and never had a boyfriend like this before so to me this was very exciting, we had stopped to eat and we sat next to each other, everyone spoke French and I didn't understand a word which was very frustrating but I was such in la la land and infatuation with Rob that at that moment I didn't even care, he would try to communicate with me using his hands as motion to talk to me and I would try to make out what he was saying, that's when I realized I had a sense of shyness in me because there was many times during that trip I felt my face turn red. I didn't want this trip to end even though my feet hurt so badly and I decided to undo my shoes in the car it was too much to handle just had to take them off, he had found that amusing.

We finally reached there house and met all the others in the family, there was so many kids there young and older, there was another woman that lived there also, it was so confusing to me but I didn't try to even understand who was who yet I was still infatuated by Rob and nothing else mattered. Everyone decided that my parents would stay at Roberts sister's house and I would stay at there house because they could get me a job right away working where Robs mom worked which was a artificial kidney plant in there town, from what I understand almost everyone from that town worked right there. I slept in the room with the other woman and she would talk to me she seemed so nice but I just couldn't understand a word of what she would say. All I wanted was to see morning as soon as possible so I could see Rob again.

A month passed and Rob would take me for walks or he would sit outside with me and draw pictures of what he was saying to better make me understand, he has never yet kissed me or anything, my heart fluttered every time we were together. He would hold my hand, give me hugs but that was it. His mother got me a job working with her there at the plant so I would leave from 7 am to 3 pm one week and the next week would be from 3 pm till 11 pm and every week it rotated that way,

I lived at Robs parents house and my parents had gotten themselves a apartment but didn't have work yet so every time I got a check I would give them money to help them out, they expected this money every payday and Robs family little by little would tell me things about my parents that would make me angry at them and I got to a point where I didn't want to give them money any more, Robs parents would convince me to keep my money saying bad things my parents were saying about me, of course I believed it. Now 18 and didn't really have to go live with them when they had asked me too and I didn't have to support them either so one day I just told them I was threw giving them money. I had the help of Robs parents always putting things in my head that would make me not want to be around my family any more. I was living a life of no violence no yelling no having to watch kids, I was free to do as I pleased in a sort of way, buy what I wanted, I loved it I got to taste freedom for just a little bit and didn't want to give it up, I was in love with a man that had just finally kissed me and his family was always so nice to me, why would I want to give that up. I started little by little to understand the French and to speak it, I know Rob loved my accent when I spoke French with that American accent and everyone at my work was getting to know me and they all called me the American. I was liked, getting popular and loved by the man I loved back so what else could I ask for, I was happy for the first time ever and I wasn't going to let anyone take that from me or away from me.

My parents had told me I had to leave there and move in with them but Robs parents made it clear that I was of age and didn't have to do anything they said anymore, and they would put bad things in my head saying my parents were saying awful things about me and it would hurt my feelings so I told them that no way was I leaving where I was, that I was happy there and I was staying. They got mad at me and stopped talking to me, what hurt the most is that I wasn't seeing my brothers and sisters and I missed them so much, I wouldn't tell anyone but at night I would cry all the time , I missed my brothers and sisters that it killed me inside, but I was in such a different world at that time I didn't even think, I wasn't going to let know one take away this happiness I was feeling. Rob and I would kiss all the time, we would sit holding each other, kisses and holds hands. I was so in love with him that nothing else existed to me, he was my world and my life, I looked forward to seeing him in the mornings and when I got off work, I loved weekends because we spent more time together, we had not yet made love to each other, I had found out threw his aunt whom was this other lady who lived there that she was Robs dad's mistress, seemed in France you can have a wife and a mistress, not that everyone was like that but he was, that explained all the kids running around, half were his and hers and the older ones were from him and Robs mom, talk about confusing but I didn't even try to sort it out or figure out who was with who or why and what, my focus was all on Rob at that time. We finally went to his brothers one weekend and they weren't there and then it happened, we had made love, It was my first time and I fell even more in love with him after that, he was just so gentle with me and was totally focused on me and how I was feeling at that time, he seen I was scared and I didn't know what to do but he made it so easy for me to trust him and I did with all my heart.

Time goes by and I'm starting to hear yelling and fighting between Robs dad and his wife and mistress, I'm so miserable, all I see is fighting and yelling on a daily basis, and I had gotten slapped a few times now from Robs mother because I didn't do something right, I missed my Family and brothers and sisters especially my brother P that lived in another town and I was being told what to do everyday from morning to dawn, I was so lonely and felt empty, Rob whom I will call Robert seemed to be the only one who was really good to me and I longed him to come home from work, he was going to have to go in the service for 2 years and I didn't want that but there was nothing I could do. I would sit for so long alone waiting, always cleaning, I felt like a maid, there wasn't much difference from them to the family I had but I still missed my family. But then again this is all I knew was to clean and do as I was told so it was kind of a normal thing for me. All I would hear was rumors they would tell me on what my family would say about me, and I was so confused but I didn't know what to believe and all I knew is that I was there with the family I had now so I had to believe whatever I was told, if I didn't I would get smacked around for it anyways so what the heck. Roberts Father would treat me pretty bad when Robert wasn't around and if I dare say anything to him he would deny it and I was the liar.

My days went on like this everyday being the same thing, I was convinced that this is the way life is, to be told what to do, when to do it, and to get slapped around. I was working at plant and going home. I would get sick in the mornings not knowing what has happened to me thinking I was sick all the time, food didn't sound good to me and sleep wasn't something I was getting accustom too. Finally going to the doctor thinking I had the bad flu I came to find out I was pregnant. I was so happy, nothing could please me more then this, and I finally had something of my very own. A child that was mine and Roberts. It was the happiest day of my life ever. Robert and I got married at the courthouse, it wasn't no wedding really and there was just family there, my parents didn't even get to come because I was brained washed by Roberts family that they didn't care about me and didn't want to see me anymore, that was real sad to me but there was nothing I could do. Threw the nine months was hard, I was always being yelled at, I was always made to do work and go to work till the last minute, but I didn't mind, all I knew is I was going to have a son and I was waiting any moment now to have him. In the meantime my parents finally got to see me and we had spent little time together but enough for us to talk and they had told me they were going back to America because it just wasn't working for them here in France. I was sad because I didn't know when I would ever see them again, and my in laws had me so brain washed against my family I was all messed up and didn't know what to do and think at that point but I knew I had to focus on me and Robert and our baby that was coming.

On July 30th 1975 at 6 am I had the most beautiful looking boy ever, he was so huge and tall. He weighed 11 pounds 5 ounces, I thought I was going to die having him, I was alone in that room, Robert was in the waiting room and I was so scared but I didn't care, my baby was worth all the pain I went threw. His name was Christophe Eric Andree and I never knew I could love such a human being. He was the light of my life, the joy of my day and the love of my life, he like saved me from being sad or lonely, he gave me the smile I never thought I would get back, he was wonderful and such a great baby, I was finally content and happy, I was so grateful that there was no words I could find to use to express the way I felt about him. I knew he was mine and a part of me that know one could ever take away from me.

Time went by, my marriage was good and my husband treated me well, I knew he loved me and he was happy with a son so my life was finally content in all ways. We had our own place in a apartment building and had made some friends but my sister in law Mauricette was my best friend, she as well wasn't well liked by the family being like me a outsider and she was treated just as bad as I was if not worse, so we stuck together all the time, I had grown to admire her strength and the care she had for our friendship, she was in deed my best friend, we would go shopping together and spend evenings drinking coffee and talking for hours. Years went by Christophe was now 5 years old and Robert my husband then wanted another child, a Daughter, I as well agreed and felt if I was going to do this I better do it now, the only thing that scared me was to have another big baby, I had got 36 stitches from the first one and 23 stitches inside of me as well because I was so torn from the birth I was just scared, back then there was no epidural or meds to help you with the pain, it was natural and as natural as they came so I was a little scared but I wanted this child real bad also and I would pray for a girl, we did all we could to try to get pregnant again. A few months past and finally I was pregnant we were happy and now hoping to have a daughter, The months went by and I was still working at the plant and caring for my son, he was such a good child I was hoping that this second one would be just as good as my son was, I was so blessed with him.

On March 18th 1981 I gave birth to a beautiful baby girl she weighed 10 pounds 7 ounces and was as perfect as they came, she had skin color of an angel and wide eyes with a smile that captured your heart. I was so happy; I had my son and my daughter and my husband thinking we were the perfect family. I had told my husband that we were threw I couldn't go threw another birth of such big children and he had agreed, my son and daughter were 6 years apart so that was good enough it was even perfect because my son was out of diapers and eating what we ate and my daughter was a all new experience yet again. I felt so blessed I had never been so happy in my whole life, I had the dream life with 2 children I loved more then life itself and I was ready to do anything for them that I could, I loved them both with a love I cant even describe it was a one of a kind love I had never felt within myself and I was never going to let go of that feeling nor ever give it away, they would come first in my life and I was willing to sacrifice whatever I had too so that they had everything they needed and then some.

Things in my marriage were starting to get a little rocky, my husband was getting so jealous and would start yelling at me a lot, I had a hard time even going to the store and if I even looked towards another man it was a fight right away. I didn't like being looked over like this I was a very faithful wife and had no interest in another man what so ever I loved my husband and my children and would never even think of wanting to be with anyone else nor even wanting to cheat with another man, I was happy, had the dream family and had no fiber in my heart to ever hurt that, but Robert was so jealous it started to cause problems in our marriage. It was his father and his family that would do it, they would tell him they seen me here or there and it was never true but I couldn't defend myself against his family they were always right to Roberts's eyes. I wanted to leave with Robert and never come back just him and my children, I knew if I got him away from his family that we would be much happier, at least I thought so. We had a 5 week vacation coming and we decided to go to America to visit my family hoping this vacation would help us and give me a break on this stress he caused me on this jealous stuff. I was so excited I was going to see my family again and they would see my children. Roberts family didn't like the idea of us going to America and especially to see my family, it's like they felt threatened or something. I didn't care what they thought or felt I wanted to go and go as soon as we could.

I had missed my family so much and all my brothers and sisters it was so good seeing them and they were very happy to see us all there with them, plus my step dad was sober and was doing really good, he was a totally different man. That's when I seen that my brother P and I had drifted apart a little but I knew we would get that back, it would just take time. I didn't want to go back to France where his family was always putting bad things in his head and always bossing me around telling me how to live my life and how to raise my children, I was never left alone they always knew everything about what we did or didn't do and it was getting to be to much for me to have them on my throat all the time I was so tired of it and being here in America I felt free, even Robert was so much better for some reason and that's when I posed the question to him asking him that we should move to America for good, that it would be great for our marriage and we wouldn't have his family on our backs all the time, he had agreed that his family was very noise and always bossed our marriage and kids around it got to the point where even Robert was fed up with his Father always telling him what to do and what I should do or not do and how to raise our kids it had got to a point that we were both tired of it and wanted out of that web, this was the perfect opportunity for us to have another chance at our marriage and a good life with our children.

We decided to not tell his family we were moving to America right away because we knew they would talk us out of it so we kept it between us only and started as soon as possible to make plans to go back, we had sold a lot of our stuff and we had made plans on a date to leave, we figured if we wait the last minute to tell his family we would be already on the way with no regret. We told his family we were leaving to live in America and I thought the end of the world was going to end. It was awful, my Father in law called me every bad name in the book and threatened to even kill me if he ever had a chance at me alone, he always gave me fear anyway because he always still hit me when Robert wasn't around and he would talk me down every chance he could so leaving this I was glad and couldn't wait, my mother in law didn't like me anyways from day one because I took her blonde headed son away from her. I can remember I had asked her why all the kids have dark brown eyes and black hair and Robert had light brown eyes and blonde hair, I had told her he looked more American then any of the boys in the family and to my belief I would of sworn that he was probably from an American back in the day when they were all in Normandy and she had slapped me in the face for even making that comment, I didn't care I was used to getting slapped around by her and her husband so it was like no big deal to me any more. There Mistress Simon was a nice lady, she felt sorry for me and she always warned me if they were in a bad mood or mad for any reason so I could just stay out of there way, what hurt the most was when my husband would be home from work they treated me like a queen, all nice to me and called me sweet names, but the minute he turned his back I was the bad step sister or should I say daughter in law, it was awful but its ok they wanted to play there games more power to them I knew I was a better person then that and I would end up being the one still smiling. Because I would never let myself get so miserable like they were, always competing, always jealous of each other, always fighting in front of my father in law and the kids grown and small, wasn't no secret they didn't like each other and to have to share the same man wasn't good either, I would just shake my head and say to myself that I would never put up with something like that if I had a husband but then again it was there choices not mine so again more power to them, I didn't care I was finally getting away from them and in a place I would be far away.

We finally move to America, lived with my parents until we could get on our feet, my dad had quit drinking so he was much better to be around, Robert had a job at a bakery and I worked for a deli, we were trying to save enough money so we could move out on our own, it was starting to get a little frustrating living at my parents house.

A couple months went by and I was wanting to move out of my parents home so bad, it just wasn't working out, Robert had changed he was so jealous all the sudden, I couldn't do anything he would get mad and I would have to justify my every move, it was getting awful and I couldn't stand it. He would argue with me at night when we were alone and get on me about my family and how I was and how he didn't like the way I dressed or things I did, but in the day when he was around my parents he was different, all nice all sweet and willing to do anything they wanted so it made me look like the bad guy if I even said anything about his behavior, know one would believe me. I took care of my children and did everything I could to please everyone just to have peace within my self. That's all I knew, I was so nieve to standing for myself or speaking up for myself that I would do as I was told, from everyone around me it was driving me crazy. We finally got ourselves a house and it was nice to have our own home I wanted that so bad, we had it set up that I worked during the day and Robert watched the kids and at night I watched them when he went to work and I was home. But the jealousy was getting worse and worse, he would come to my work during the day and watch me to see if I flirted with other men or to watch how I was around other people, it was so awful for me, the last thing I knew is how to even do anything wrong I was always scared of every person, place or thing. There were endless nights when he would keep me up

31

yelling at me because I looked at some guy a certain way and I didn't even know I did, or if I spoke to a customer to long he thought I was flirting and it was starting to be just to much. I had told my mom about it but she didn't believe me, Robert could do no wrong to her eyes, he was the best thing I ever had is what she always said, and at some point there was the hidden ways he had, know one but I knew so I had to live with it and I was miserable.

Robert had decided he didn't want to stay in America any more that we needed to go back to France. I about died when he told me that and I just couldn't do that to myself again there was no way I was going to go back to that life again there was no way, and I wasn't about to put my children in that situation. I let him know that I didn't want to go back, we would fight about it every night, he said he would go back alone to find us a place and get us settled then when he got back I was to be ready to leave. So he had decided to go for a visit for a few weeks on his own just to visit his family and he had a plan but I didn't know what that plan was until later. While he was gone to France I was good, I took care of the kids I worked and I never ever once flirted or seen another man, it wasn't me, I was a very faithful woman and I feared to much doing anything like that anyways it just didn't even cross my mind, it wasn't something I even thought of, I was that dedicated to my marriage. But I guess when Robert was in France for that visit it wasn't the same thing in his mind, oh yes he wanted to get me back to France and away from the American life so he could have more and better control over my life without family getting in the way or anyone else but while he was there he seemed to have a eye on a mutual friend we had her name was Patricia and she had always had a crush on Robert from when we lived in France so when she seen him there alone she took fully advantage on what she felt was a future gain for herself. I found out threw my sister in law that Robert was hanging out with Patricia day and night, my sister in law had heard they had an affair and seen this so she had called me and told me everything. It hurt me so bad that I had all the sudden lost a sense of love I thought I had for him, I mean I still loved him but I wasn't in love with him any more.

While he was away I was able to get up when I wanted go to bed when I wanted come and go as I pleased and this was to me a whole new life,

I felt free, for the first time in my whole life I felt so free, I did what I wanted without having to answer to anyone but myself and it felt so good. I would look in the mirror and say to myself, oh my god is this what you call freedom of ones self? It confused me but then again it let me know I liked it, I had never had this I had never been able to do what I wanted when I wanted and how I wanted, I didn't answer to know one and it was nice, I ate what I wanted and when I wanted I was like a little girl with a new toy. But yet I also stayed very faithful, even the kids seemed happier because we did things together and they never heard yelling so to them it was fun to be with mommy. And then he came back and here I was once again answering to all his beck and calls and arguing with him because of him being jealous.

I even didn't want to be with him no more knowing he had been with another woman and he didn't know I knew. I wanted that freedom back that two weeks I spent of what I called freedom of my life and loving it, oh I wanted this back so much that the more he would yell at me and start hitting on me the more I would start to get stronger with myself to finally one day have the courage to put my foot down. But every time I thought I had the courage I backed out, I was scared, he would hit me in the face if I would do something wrong like cook to much or to hot or not hot enough or I didn't have the house clean enough or the kids were making noise, it didn't matter every time I turned around I was getting a slap in the face or a thump on the head, that fear alone would never give me the courage to tell him I wanted to leave him I was just to scared, he was a great father to the kids but he just didn't want me for his wife and I knew it he wanted that other woman.

One day when he went to far and he had hit me so bad, kicked me and I hit back this time, it was awful that I got so scared I called my mom right as we were fighting so she could hear it for herself and for the first time she took my side, it was a feeling of relief, a beginning for me of strength a way to let myself know that I can do this I just have to be strong and I can do this, so I told him I wanted him to leave and I didn't want to be with him any more, he was shocked that I could even think of that but I stood my ground and told him I had had enough and I wanted out of this marriage. He went to my family's house and stayed there a few days and decided to go back to France to think things out and hope I would do the same. I couldn't wait to get that freedom feeling again I was longing for it and wasn't ready to let nothing get in the way of me being alone with my children for the first time in my life and be free of any man telling me what to do or hitting me or abusing me. No more I was going to be free to make my own choices and do what ever I wanted when ever I wanted and I just couldn't wait.

My new freedom

Robert had left to go back to France and while he was gone I decided to file for divorce, my mother and dad finally believed me when I told them the stuff I had put up with and finally they took my side and stood by me, that was a start for me to get strong and be a woman that can do this on her own without having to be told what to do all the time, a couple months had gone by and I had papers drawn up on our divorce. I had also met a friend this guy that would come by my work all the time he was nice and very kind, I would never go out with him because I was scared but to just feel like someone wanting me was a special feeling, something new and something I had not had in a long time and I liked that feeling of being wanted or liked by another man. His name was mike and we started to see each other a lot but I still wouldn't kiss him nor let him touch me we just spent time together and talked a lot we laughed he was just real nice to me and I really enjoyed that a lot.

I had moved out of the house and got myself a apartment closer to my parents, I had the kids in school I had a new job working in a office for a cabinet maker and I was really happy. When I moved in my apartment the manager there was real nice, he was a single father with two little girls he was raising on his own, I would leave in the mornings and he would stand out side with a cup of coffee and always waved bye to me as I left for work every morning. So I was actually flirting with him and with mike and to be honest it felt real good, I felt like I was special but I never did anything like kiss or touch I just flirted with them both. One night mike calls me and wanted to come see me so I said yes, my kids were asleep and I felt good about letting him come over to see me. I had made coffee and we sat there and talked and then it happened he kissed me, it had gotten dark and the lights were turned off except one and one thing led to another and we started to get very touchy with each other kissing when all the sudden I hear a pound on my door and I hear Roberts voice saying to open the door. I was so scared, what was he doing here he was supposed to be in France, he had come back and not told anyone, he had found out where I was and from what I understand he was watching me that night, when he seen that man go into my apartment he waited until he saw there was hardly no lights turned on and he went nuts. I told mike he had to hurry and just leave that I was very afraid and I didn't want problems, I told mike that it was my soon to be ex husband and he was very jealous and I was afraid he was going to hurt me or him.

He wanted to call the police and I begged him not too that I could handle Robert and I made him promise me to just go and not call the police and to just let me handle the situation that I knew how to handle Robert myself. So mike left and I locked the door, it wasn't two minutes later that Robert started to pound on the door again saying to me to open the door and I would tell him threw the door to go away and we will talk in the morning, then I hear the cops and Robert took off. They came to my door saying they had received a call saying I might be in danger, I had told them it was my soon to be ex and everything was ok I wasn't going to have Robert thrown in jail I just wouldn't do that so they finally left when I refused to press charges they didn't know where Robert was because he had left before they got there and I had no idea where he was even staying. I laid on the couch that night hearing noises and couldn't sleep at all I was scared Robert was out there but I wasn't going to open that door for nothing so I knew I was safe, I didn't tell my parents until the next day. My mother was so upset to hear that he had done that and asked if I needed to come stay with them, I knew Robert wasn't going to hurt me, I knew he was just real jealous and he didn't know yet that I had divorce papers waiting for him, it had been six months sense he had left I didn't think he would even ever come back.

The next day he calls me and asked if he could come see me I agreed to see him at my parents house with the kids so he did, come to find out he had just got in from France a few days before and he had watched me leave my parents home to my home and that's how he knew where I lived, he was nice when we met and the kids were so happy to see him, they didn't know what was going on all they knew was that daddy was gone. We spoke and I let him know I had divorce papers ready for him, he wasn't happy because he said he had come back in hopes we would give it another try at our marriage. I wasn't willing to even consider it, I got that taste of freedom and doing as I wish and I wasn't willing to give that up. So he said he was going to stay for just a few weeks and go back to France if he could see the kids and spend time with them, I had no problem with that after all he was a good father to them when he was around. During those few weeks that Robert was there I had found out threw a friend that mike the great man I had met was married, he had lied to me and told me he was single, I was hurt so I called mike and told him I didn't ever want to see him again that I knew he was married and if he tried to bother me I would call his wife, I was never bothered by him again. Robert had asked me if he could use my car one day while I was at work so I said yes, he just needed it to get his ticket in order for when he was leaving back to France. He was being real good and nice the time he was here and didn't bother me at all. What I didn't realize was he had the keys to my apartment on my car keys and he had gone to my apartment and went threw everything he could think of, what was he looking for I have no idea I had nothing to hide but he was looking for evidence of if I had a man staying there with me or not, the way I found out was he had brought me back my car like he had said I had dropped him off at his hotel and went home, the minute I walked in I knew he had been there he wore this cologne that I would never forget and it smelled like him as soon as I walked in the door, I went threw the house and knew he had gone threw my clothes my drawers everything in the bathroom and in my drawers in the closet, I thought he had maybe set up a camera or something so I went to see my manager sense I had heard he was a private investigator for workers comp I figured he could help me. I knocked on his door he opens the door with a baby in his arms which was his daughter who was only 3 months old, he invites me in and of course I pay attention to the baby and the little girl playing at the table that was about 2 years old. I proceed to tell him what had happened and he said yes I will come up there and check everything for you, he gathers up the girls and he followed me to my apartment which was just above his. He hands me the baby and starts going threw my apartment and lets me know that no he probably just went threw stuff because there was nothing left or planted there so I was safe. He was real nice telling me the kids mother was gone and he was raising them alone and he was a investigator as well as the manager, I was so impressed to see such a man doing all this on his own, he was tall, to me he was good looking and he was very nice, he would tell me how he had noticed me and he would go out on purpose in the mornings just to wave at me, it made me smile and again feel like I was special, we talked for a while he invited me and the kids to come eat with him and the girls. We did and the night ended in a thank you. As I walked out of there gong towards my apartment with my 2 children, holding there hands and smiling at them. I had no idea that from that point on, things were about to change for the rest of my life.

I served Robert with his divorce papers. I loved him so much but what he didn't know was that Patricia had called me from the first time he went to France to visit and she had told me that they had slept together, it killed me, broke my heart, she then followed by telling me he had told her that he didn't love me and that he wanted to be with her, I had hung up the phone but the calls continued and she kept telling me how if I said anything that he would take my kids away from me and take them to France. So I never told him about her calls because I believed her when she told me they slept together that he was hers and that if I did anything to keep him back she would have my kids as well as him and as heart broken as I was I divorced him, he at one point told me he wanted us to get back together but I thought it was because he wanted to get back so he could leave with the kids so I had told him no. He never knew how much I loved him, he was like the love of my life and I was so heart broken I cried for days, it took me a long time to love again even years, I would be with a guy but that love would never come back and I was convinced that I would never again get married because no matter what I still loved Robert so much and couldn't even tell him because of what Patricia had told me, so I just kept it to myself and went the other way, and he left to go back to France and I never seen him again. Patricia would taunt me with calls telling me she was going to have Roberts baby and on and on until I finally changed my number so I didn't have to hear from her again, my Divorce papers said he had to pay child support for the children but he never did, he never knew about Patricia's calls to me and he never looked back. It was so sad because he just had no idea how much I really loved him and how much I hurt from all the stuff Patricia had told me that I just had to let him go, I had believed that if I didn't let him go that I would lose my kids and him so if it meant letting him go and keeping my kids then I had to do what I had to do, but I never till this day ever told him about all her calls and how mean she was and the threats about having my kids taken away if I didn't divorce him, so I did, heart broken and all I did what I thought was best for my kids and for me. Bill would continue to talk to me and meet me outside when the kids were playing, this continued on for a few weeks.

It's amazing how you think you know everything or everyone around you and you really don't even have a clue until something happens then you ask yourself "why". I was what you call a naive woman that all she knew was to take care of people and kids, to work all the time and sacrifice whatever I had for my kids. My worse default was I believed what I was told so badly that it hurt me in many ways.

Time went on that Bill would romance me with flowers and dinners along with using the kids he had to attract me to him and it worked, he gave my kids games and a lot of attention also and that's all it took, he would tell me all about how my freedom from my husband was the best thing I ever did and that I was a good strong woman when all in all deep inside I was weak and had no clue what I was about to do or have done to me.

I was working for this cabinet shop as a secretary and I liked it a lot, my boss kept telling me that the man I was about to move in with was a user and no good, that he was manipulating me to get what he wants, when I asked what was it he wanted he answered me " I'm not sure yet but it isn't good" but I was blinded by the romance I was being given, and I wasn't accustom too it so I wouldn't listen , even my step father told me that there was something about bill he didn't like and he was afraid that bill was about to ruin my life but then again I didn't listen, I thought know one see's when we are alone and he is so nice to me, how he makes me feel like im the best woman on this earth until that night finally came. It had been a few months now we had been seeing each other and he had talked me into moving in with him which I did, his family was so nice but know one yet knew his secret so I felt so welcomed by everyone even though my family didn't approve with the move but I did it anyways. One thing I didn't think was normal was on the weekends there were so many people at our house, in the bedrooms bathrooms kitchen everywhere, I would keep the kids in one room and I would stay with them until everything started to Seattle down. I did notice that all the sudden my brother, was becoming bills best friend who was odd to me but I never asked questions. The weekends started to turn into 4 days a week then all week, I know there was something not right but I was so naive that I still didn't ask until one night there was a guy in the bathroom laying on the floor shaking and foam was coming out of his mouth, I sneaked out of the room the kids were all sleeping and I kept the light off, as I walked into the hall I could see bill and another guy picking up this man and putting him in the shower with cold water, as they did so I seen blood on the floor and a syringe. When bill turned his head and seen I was watching he yelled at me and ordered me to go back in the bedroom with the kids so I did. About a hour later seemed everyone had left, even the guy that was in the shower, all there was left was my brother and bill, I slowly come out there in the kitchen and I see syringes and white substance on the table with all kinds of contraband from that party but I yet had no clue what it was all used for, that's when bill hands me a cup of Pepsi to drink he said drink this and sit down I need to explain something to you, I did as I was told but I was asking him who was that guy I seen that they put in the shower and what's all this stuff and what's going on, but all he would say was just sit down drink this and shut up I will explain, so I did, within a few minutes I had drank my Pepsi I was so thirsty from being in that room for so long but then I felt funny, I felt like the room was starting to blur and when he spoke it seemed like he was far away, he had asked me if he could make me feel better and I had said yes because I didn't know what I was doing, I remember he put something around my arm then I seen the syringe in his hand and then within minutes I felt like I was in another world, like I was harmless, know one could hurt me or get to me, it was a feeling of safety and happiness it was a feeling I didn't want to see go away, I remember sitting there in a blah and just not even caring what was going on around me or what bill was saying I know I felt great and then I fell asleep.

I wake up the next morning I was in the bed naked, not knowing what happened nor what I did, I couldn't even remember my name, I didn't know where I was and who everyone was around me, their kids were all out of the room and I didn't even know where I was, I get up and bill is sitting in the other room and says to me, mom has the kids for the day so you can rest, I was like what's going on and what happened to me, I remember he sat me down and gave me some coffee to drink and as time went by I was starting to remember who and where I was, then I started to get upset and ask him what the hell did he do to me and where were the kids and where were MY kids, he grabs my coffee cup puts more coffee in it and hands it to me says to me drink this and I will explain. As I waited for him to tell me what was going on I was hurting so bad, my gut hurt and my body hurt, my head was about to explode and I felt so sick to my stomach and ran to the bathroom to throw up…"I was a victim of a date rape drug but didn't even know it" along with other drugs I had no clue yet what was about to happen…when I got back he says drink the coffee and I did, it wasn't 2 minutes as I drank I started to feel all better, that quick, no more headache no more body pain and not sick to my stomach, it was like it all went away within a minute, I still never realized he had put something in my coffee cup, I wasn't out of it this time I was awake well aware of my surroundings and felt great, like better then normal and he sits down to explain to me that all these people that he would have over were people that worked undercover with him for the workforce institution he was with and it was drugs I seen on the table and they were testing them out to make sure they was dealing with the right dealers ect ect ect, I didn't have a clue what he was telling me because I didn't understand any of it but I went along with what ever he said because the way I was feeling this time I would of agreed with whatever you told me. At work my boss said to me that he was seeing something was wrong, I had lost a lot of weight in that few weeks and I just wasn't the same, he kept telling me he was worried about me but I always reassured him that I was just fine.

Weeks passed and as a daily thing bill made my coffee everyday when I got up and I felt great. What ever it was he was giving me it didn't affect with my daily routine because I would do even more then I ever thought I could. Take care of the 4 kids clean house work cook and party, it was great like super woman. He continued to have his friends there weekly there were people in and out of our house day and night it had become a custom to me and I just stayed with the kids in the bedroom with the TV on so to me it wasn't bad, I know he always made sure I always had something to drink until one day I didn't drink his coffee and I got so sick, sick to where I couldn't care for the kids couldn't get out of bed and couldn't even function, my brother had come over to visit and he said I needed to get better and he had what I needed, he brings out this white substance and puts it in my drink, to that point I was willing to let anyone do whatever it took just so I got better, and it wasn't a minute after he gave me that, I was all better, like magic, I was able to move round like nothing ever happened I was without pain and felt like the whole world was at my mercy, that's when my friend whom also showed up told me that bill had been drugging me on a daily basis so I wouldn't say anything about all the activity going on in and out of our house and that's when I knew I wasn't going to make it unless I had that drug everyday, I was hooked before I even knew what hooked meant. When bill came home that day I told him I knew what he had done to me and what was happening when he gave me coffee everyday or drinks of Pepsi that was filled with heroin. I was addicted to heroin and I didn't even know what this drug did to you except that it made me feel safe and strong willed, I could conquer the world with no pain what so ever. This went on for months now and I was doing drugs like six weeks until the worse happened, the girls that belonged to bill were given back to there mom and my kids had to be sent to there father in France because I had no way of taken care of them and I thought they would be better off with him until I got my life together. It was only supposed to be temporary and I believed it, that was the hardest thing I ever did was tell my children that they had to go to France to visit there dad until mommy could get things back together and mommy could care for them again. They were sad but as well excited, they were small so they didn't know any better they thought they were going to see daddy for a vacation. Watching them get on the plane and seeing them leave was a sad day for me but I knew they would be back real soon so I as well took it as they were going on vacation to see there daddy.

After all this was done and we had no kids around I was fired from my job for stealing, Bill and I had stole checks from my boss and made them out to my brother or to a friend to get money to pay the rent or to buy drugs, come to find out bill was fired long ago from his job as a private investigator for workers comp and he never got another job he was a drug dealer period and I had just figured that out. I sat there in tears thinking he talked me into letting my kids go to there father so I could better our life for them and he let his kids go but it was all just to get rid of them so he had freedom to wheel and deal without no kids in the way, I cried so much that day realizing I had just thrown away my life and my kids, I felt so bad and didn't know what to do next, I was lost and had no idea how I was going to make it anymore.

Soon enough that day was going to change my life, I was cleaning the house sad about my kids missing them so much it would kill me and I came across the closet where there was boots that belonged to bill, I pull them out because I had seen this bag in them, I pulled out the bag and it was full of this white substance which to be honest I thought it was stuff to make your boots smell good except there was no smell, I thought it was pretty strange so I took it out and laid it on the kitchen table and went about my house cleaning, I hear a knock on the door and when I opened it there stood my step dad who would come over and see me a few times a week just to visit, he knew I missed my kids and he knew something wasn't right but he hadn't yet figured it out. He was sober now for like 10 years so he would do everything he could to be a dad to me and make up for all the bad years, and I liked him sober, he was kind and understanding, I knew it was all a little to late to start being a dad but why not give him that chance, after all I wanted a dad anyways so we got along real well. Anyways when I let him in he seen the bag on the table as I was making him coffee and he said to me "what's this" and I tell him exactly what I thought and I said " that's stuff that came out of bill's boots so I took it out", he said to me you have no idea what this is do u and I said no why, as I hand him his coffee he opened the bag and smelled it then he took a taste of a tiny bit of the powder there was and he says to me this belongs to bill ? And I said yes why, he says hand me the phone so I did and a few minutes later I get a knock on my door whom was the cops, they come in my dad shows them the bag and they asked me where I go it, I tell them and they search my house and right in the same place I found the bag they pull up the carpet and there sat all this money in bundles and all these bundles of pot. How would I of known and even more I didn't even know what all that stuff was, I was so naive to this stuff that it was sickening, a full grown woman and didn't even have a clue to what was about to happen to her life and to think I had it bad to this point but wasn't even ready for what was about to happen in the future to come.

My dad's intentions was not to have me put in jail but to have Bill put in jail, but I was taken to jail on possession of drugs and they looked for Bill as well while they looked for him they questioned me and realized that I had no clue what was going on, they had caught bill and they let me go, knowing that I really didn't know what was going on. I get a call from him and of course I bail him out not knowing what else to do because he was all I had he was my boyfriend he was the one who said he loved me and he didn't abuse me like the other men in my life. When he got home he sat me down and explained to me what was really going on, I didn't know how to take it because I still didn't really understand, my brother would come over a lot and bring his wife because we would all get high together so it was free for them, they both decided that I might as well join them to be a part of them I guess so after explaining to me about cocaine and heroin they decided to show me more of what it did, my brother held my arm and bill used a needle to inject me with this liquid, I let them do it because I knew no better and just wanted to be a part of, after getting that injection I felt like I had before when I used to drink the coffee, I felt no pain, no fear and felt like know one would ever hurt me again, the feeling went threw my veins so fast and it made me sleepy yet again made me hyper both at the same time. I remember looking at my brother and bill and they said to me see it's all good huh "do you like it" my answer to them was but of course I like it if it makes you feel Like you're the strongest person on earth with no fears left no worries and no pain. From that point on I was hooked and I didn't want to feel that fear anymore. This was going to be my new way of life.

Watching life from the inside out

It came time to going to court for the charges on the drugs found in my home and I had just found out I was pregnant. When I told bill and my family everyone wanted me to have a abortion but in my gut something told me to not go threw with it that I needed this child that I loved this child and here I was hooked on drugs so I went to a friend and they gave me pills to get over the drugs so I could have a normal pregnancy and after 4 weeks I was almost drug free but I still took pills to take the edge off as they called it, and by that time I was 7 months pregnant I was so scared. Bill had convinced me that if I took the blame for the drugs found in our home and didn't involve him at all that I would get a slap on the hand and sent home because I had a clean record and being pregnant they would feel sorry for me in the courts, so I believed him and went over and over with him the night before court what I was going to say in court, he had told me he loved me and I believed that, he told me he would be there for me and I believed that also and he said I would have a father for our child whom we knew was a boy and I also believed that as well.

The morning of court I was so nervous because my step father was there and a lot of people I knew would be there, as I stood in front of the judge I remember him asking me all these questions and I would answer them exactly the way bill had gone over it with me, the judge had asked me, " are you sure you are not here saying your guilty to protect anyone else" as I looked towards the floor I would say no Sir I'm not, I couldn't lie to know ones face so I would look towards the ground when I told a lie, the judge for some reason didn't believe me and had asked me again are you sure? And again I had said No Sir. It all went so fast I didn't know what to think he hits that wooden hammer on his desk and sentences me to 3 five year consecutive to serve at Oregon state Woman Prison and to start the time right away. I remember standing there in such shock I was numb and I slowly turn my head to see if I could see bill there and all I seen was his back as he was walking out the courtroom, then I looked at my step dad and he had the saddest look on his face it killed me, I feel handcuffs hit my hands and I was taken away to a cell to await my trip to prison, I about fainted not even knowing what just happened to me, I was like in a blank not knowing what was going on everything was blurry and the voices that spoke to me were like far away, I think I was having a panic attack and didn't know it.

Four days later at 4 am in the morning I was asked to roll it up I was going to be transported to Salem. By 6 am I was in a bus 7 months pregnant and on my way to prison not knowing what I was about to face, I was so scared all I did was cry. I thought to myself how could he just let me take the fall and leave like he did, how could he just abandon me like that and why, I just didn't understand but it was to late to try to understand anything now it was done and I was going to do the time. I arrived at the Oregon's Women's correctional Center and all I could see was chain link fences with barb wire on top and guard's all over, I was lead threw a hall way to be possessed and put in a waiting room to be checked by a nurse before I was put into the public as they called it. I remember a few women walking by making these sounds like "oh a milky one" or "oh a new piece of meat" I was so scared I started to shake, the nurse came in she was very nice but stern and said if your going to be here for 5 years you better get used to that and over look the comments, she checked me out and said I was healthy took a blood test to see if I had drugs in my system which I didn't and she said well your off to a good start, now keep your nose clean and mind your own business and you will get threw this like a piece of cake. "easy for her to say" I was then took to a room where I was alone at first, there was a 4x4 small window at the top of the wall and big locks on the door, the guard was nice to me and said don't be afraid because the long timers here prey on fear. I was so lost I still wondered why I was here but a little to late for that.

I had no visitors except my step dad, he would come see me once a week or when he could, my family had disowned me and I had no friends and as for bill he was long gone. It was lunch time and I was told to go eat in the lunch room which I did, the noise was loud and the women looked so mean so I found myself a little corner to sit at alone, I remember we had Mac n cheese with a cinnamon roll and choice of milk or juice. As I sat there trying to eat this arm reaches down to take the cinnamon roll right off my plate, I was so scared I didn't move and let her do it as she laughed. God what was I about to go threw in in this place. I pretty much stayed to myself but I watch every movement around me, I would always sit with my back to the wall, never give anyone the opportunity to sneak up behind me again. I seen more drugs then I ever did on the outside and the cussing was awful with these women but I always stayed quiet. This woman approached me she was about 60 years old and there for murder but she was so sweet you would have never known she was a murder; she sat by me one day and started to talk to me. Mail was handed out and I had a letter from someone I didn't even know so I opened it and started to read it as this lady kept talking, she waited until I finished reading my letter which was very short, all it said was "I will get you out of there princess, just have some faith and I will send for you" and it was signed "your future".

This lady started to talk to me again, I never answered I just listened as she told me, you need to not be so nieve and quiet because you're a perfect target for the bullies in here, she proceeded to let me know what goes on in there and what to do and not to do, and who to not piss off. To be honest I didn't care I just wanted to be left alone and alone is what I stayed, I hardly came out of my room only for meals and to go out side when needed just to get some fresh air, and take showers. There were these girls in a group of 5 that always made comments to me but I ignored them, they would watch my every move when I did come out of my room which wasn't often except to see my visitor which was always the same person, my step dad. But least I had him. I had been there now 2 months and it was early I was in the shower and all the sudden the shower curtain fly's open and there was the 5 girls that always hung out they had a test tube in there hands and had told me they need me to pee in it, I was like "NO" and they told me they needed it for a drug test and they knew I was clean so all I needed to do was pee in it and they were done with me, but I didn't want to do that I didn't want nothing to do with them or anything they was doing so when I refused they told me its either pee in it or pay the consequence. I didn't believe them until they started to hit me and punch me in the stomach, punch my face until finally 3 guard's came to me and stopped it. By that time I was pretty beat up, I was taken to the nurses office where I was checked out because I was now 8 months pregnant and didn't know if there was any damages to my baby or not, I was taken to the hospital and after getting exam med the baby was just fine, I had a black eye and a sprained arm and burses all over but nothing I couldn't get over. From then on I made sure to keep my eyes out on what was said and done around me, I couldn't believe how some inmates got away with things they never should of then again some inmates were being abused to a extent that there was no reason for it but know one believed them and the bullies got away with it, it was sad and sick to see how preference was being done but then again I didn't care as long as I was left alone that's all I wanted so I stayed to myself except for Ola the old lady who seemed to love talking to me, she was sweet and had great words of wisdom for being in prison, I liked her after a while and her words spoken were wise ones to remember, she would tell me how its not worth being in there for someone else's crime and how to not let people push u around, she taught me how to be strong in mind and wise in my actions and so I listened to her, not only did it help pass the time but it taught me what not to be when I would get out.

I ended up really liking her, she was so nice I just couldn't believe she was there for murder, she had told me she had taken one to many beatings and to her it was worth spending time in prison then to watch him start hitting the kids.

Two and a half months there I remember I was visiting with my step dad and you could see people coming in to visit there family when I seen this man walk in and we made eye contact, he looked so familiar but at the time I just couldn't place where I had seen him before but that look I would never forget, he spoke to one of the guards she slightly looked my way then turned to him as they spoke he left but as he walked out he gave me that grin the kind you never forget. My step dad was still talking and going on about the family, while he was talking he didn't even realize I had glanced away from him to see this mans look. When my visit was over and we had to go threw a shake down I had asked the guard who was that man, she seemed uncomfortable answering me and said was just a good friend to the warden, I had told her I knew him from somewhere but couldn't place my hand on it but I had seen him before, that his look was one I had never forgot I just couldn't place it. She had told me that I was wrong and to just forget it. I can remember that night as I was laying in my bunk I had that mans look in my head, but where did I remember him from, I know I knew him I felt it but I just couldn't remember where. That night I remember the prayers I would always ask God and for the first time I had realized that when I prayed I asked God for strength, that I might achieve but I was made weak, that I might learn humbly to obey. I asked for health that I might do greater things, but I was given infirmity, that I might do better things. I asked for riches that I might be happy, but I was given poverty that I might be wise, I asked for power that I might have the praise of men but I was given weakness that I might feel the need of God, I asked for all things that I might enjoy life, but I was given life, that I might enjoy all things. So in reality I got nothing I had asked for but everything I had hoped for, Almost despite myself, my unspoken prayers were answered, I am among all most richly blessed. I laid there until I fell into a deep sleep almost like so deep I felt like I was falling into a dark hole...

The Dream

Nine months pregnant entering My third month there at about 5 pm I was called to the wardens office and was asked to have a seat, when I did I was told about someone special in my life had just proven my innocence and I was going to be released first thing in the morning, that all charges were cleared and I was free and that someone will be here to pick me up and take care of all the proper procedures for me to have what I need. I was so happy I started to cry, was this for real, was I really getting to leave and who was this special person that did this and who was coming to get me, all they said was they will be waiting out side when you get out first thing in the morning. I didn't argue I was so excited I didn't even sleep, all I did was wait for that door to pop open so I could leave, come 6 am the door opened and the guards escorted me to the front door wishing me luck and telling me to never come back, with my excitement I told them not to worry they will never see me again.

When I walked out the tall big doors I seen a big black car, nice shinny and four men standing by it with smiles on there faces. I was like wait, who are you and what this is. They told me don't be afraid that everything was ok and to just get in the car, that they would take me to the designated area they were supposed to take me. As always I did as I was told and got in the car, the three men were very nice, here I am 9 months pregnant and in a car with total strangers not even knowing where I was going, now how dumb was that but I was again so damn naive I did as I was told. And once again no matter what the consequences all I knew is I was out of that prison place. They were very nice to me asking me if I was thirsty or hungry they had fresh water with them and even sandwiches and they assured me I was safe and they were the good guys to just wait and see, so I did, I would just say ok no problem and wait to see where I was going, After about a 2 hour drive we finally get to the designated area. We drive up a long driveway which crosses a small bridge with a nice little river then up this hill until you see this beautiful shallot cabin looking home that was just beautiful, a huge log cabin in the middle of know where and it was just amazing how beautiful it was.

As we drove to the front of the house they stopped the car and opened my door saying just go on in, there is someone there waiting for you? I thought to myself who on earth would I know that would help me like this, I know that there were so many times that I seemed to get away with things, or if I did without in the streets all the sudden I would have a place to stay and always food to eat and to my knowledge I always thought I had the best guardian angel ever. As I got to the door I opened it to inter in a huge living area that was just beautiful, Indian style pictures on the wall, leather couch and chairs, oak table and chairs in the dinning area, open beam walls and ceiling's and very well kept. As I stood there I hear a voice, deep voice that said to me "turn around princess" as I turned around I see this tall man with dark eyes and long eyelashes holding this doll in his hands. I just froze thinking to myself "this is the man I seen when I was a little girl in France that my mother sent away" As I looked at him he smiled at me and said have a seat we have a lot to talk about, I had asked him "who are you" and his response was please sit and we will talk. He was so handsome and had that Steven Segal look to him except he had tattoo's all over his arms, I watched him walk towards his desk as he lead me to the office and I noticed he had the name princess on his arm, he had just called me that and I had no clue who he was, as I sat in this huge chair that was so comfortable he sits across me at his desk and says to me, "I don't want to scare you nor do I want you to think I am going to hurt you because I will never do that" then he proceeds to tell me he was my father, my real father. His nick name was Tony, He was kept away from me all these years and I had never known but he had told me that the last few years he had finally found me and he kept a eye out for me, he had told me how he felt I was very naive and allowed other's to take advantage of me or that I was so lonely I felt I just had to have these kinds of people because I just didn't know any better. He started to talk about my mother to let me know this was for real and it wasn't a joke. All the things he would say about my mother and my grandfather in France with details threw out my life led me to believe he was telling me the truth. He hands me the doll he had 24 years before when I was six that was thrown back at him by my mother and said, "I kept this hoping it would help you remember that day and this doll I had brought you" he spoke no bad about her all he would say she had made some bad choices and she had paid her price threw out her life that there was no sense in wanting to feel anger, he had told me that he still loved her for giving him a beautiful girl even though he didn't get the chance to watch me grow up or was allowed to be near me he always made sure he would have some information on my behalf to always make sure I was ok, he knew I went threw a very hard time that I was left alone a lot in my young years that he suspected abuse in more ways then one but his hands were tied at that time, that he knew this day was going to happen so he felt it was best to wait. He had told me he didn't plan on us meeting this way but he couldn't take it any longer to watch me suffer and especially being pregnant. He wasn't going to let me suffer no more so he had people he knew in high places as well as low places and he had gathered enough evidence to prove to the courts I was innocent of the crime I was sent to prison for, he had said it just took longer then he had expected and this is why he was just now able to get me out. Mean while he let me know how much he loved me and missed me, he told me about seeing me every year of my life until these last few years when I decided to hit the wrong path, he had told me I was hard to keep up with. He then says to me lets eat and we can continue this conversation, he said do you have any questions. As I looked at him I softly said, not yet but I will, I just want to listen first then I will ask my questions, he says to me ok enough. He gets up and says I want to introduce you to your brothers, they were the four men that had picked me up, and to think I had no clue who they even were. He says this is Johnny, Michael, Lee and Jake; there your older brothers and you my dear child are my only daughter and the baby waiting to have a baby herself. I looked at him and I would like be amazed by his look and his eyes its almost like he could read right threw you but then again he had this safe look that made you feel like its going to be ok. So I just said hi in a very polite way and followed Tony towards the kitchen to eat, he had dinner ready with potatoes beef and greens along with salad, he told me to make myself at home because as of now this was my home. I looked at him and said, how long do you plan on keeping me here, he looks at me and says until we are threw talking, and that all my questions are answered, then he was going to let me know what he had planned and if I was ok with it, I was welcome to stay as long as I wanted but if I felt this wasn't what I wanted then he would take me anywhere I wanted to go. I turned towards the table to sit down and eat as I thought to myself where else do I have to go, my family except my step dad had disowned me, I had no friends and had know where to go, so I might as well finish this meeting as I called it for now and go from there, I had to many questions to ask and I needed answers to so many things, I was so lost at this point but I also felt really safe like something in me was saying just do this and see what he has to offer as well as answering all my questions. As we were eating I stayed pretty quiet and I watched the guys talk with each other and laugh and joke like a real family but I knew the authority came from Tony because when he spoke the guys would give him there attention in a very respectful way. I seen Tony look at me as well as the guys and they didn't ask me anything or bother me with how I am how I was what I want or need, they just kept it like I was just a part of the family and would give me eye contact when they spoke about things they did or about the land what they did here and I just listened. After dinner Tony told Johnny to take me to where my room was that I probably wanted to freshen up and get relaxed a little bit. As I started to walk behind Johnny Tony says to me, after you have rested and made yourself comfortable you let me know when you are ready to continue this talk and I will be here for you, at anytime of the day or night. I looked at him and said "Thank you". When I walked in my room Johnny said to me, don't worry it's going to be just fine I promise you ok, he smiles and walks away. I was so tired and so confused at this time I went to the bed and just laid down, my baby was moving to much I was just tired. I had fallen asleep. I wake up and its already dark, I can hear the guys down the hall in the living room talking and laughing but not loud to where that had woke me up, I get up and I see clothes in the closet, with shoes and drawers full of socks underwear and everything I needed, I was like how did they even know. On the dresser there was a picture of the 4 boys and Tony then to the side there was a frame with pictures of me from when I was little until like a few years ago. I couldn't believe it, there was even a picture of me and Tony when I was 20 at this picnic and didn't even know who he was but some how I had my picture taken with him, how amazing all this was. I walked to the bathroom and there is all I need for hygiene as in shampoo lotion make-up even my favorite perfume from Victoria secrets. I was just amazed at all this and how did they know to get me everything I needed, there were things there that I thought were so nice and pretty as in my clothes and shoes everything. I decided I needed a shower and got myself freshened up, looking at my self I was in my first week of my nine months pregnant and I was just so fat, at least that's how I felt. There was a pair of sweats that fit me perfect and they were so comfortable I just couldn't believe it, I got dressed, put on some makeup and felt so much better, I was rested and now wide awake. It was all the sudden quiet down the hall but I needed to get me something to drink I was thirsty, so I open my door and look out and didn't see anyone, I walked down the hall towards the kitchen and opened the fridge to find lots of different juices to drink even yogurt and fresh fruit, so I get me a orange and peel it, I got me a glass of orange juice had a paper towel with me and started to walk back towards the dinning room, I looked at the pictures on the wall, at the way it was decorated then I walked to the living area and it was just so huge but so nice, I could smell the leather from the couch and chairs, the pictures on the wall were so amazing and so pretty, pictures of horses and Indians and the dessert it was all just really nice, I even remembered when I was in TJ's office all I had seen there was Harley Davidson's and pictures of riders and lots of motorcycle style stuff. As I opened the glass doors that went out to a balcony I wanted to smell the fresh air, as I stood there drinking my orange juice and eating my orange I felt very good, and for some reason very safe, I hear a voice behind me that had scared me that had said "how are you feeling" I kind of jumped a little but not much I was just startled and there stood TJ, he was so handsome and tall with the most beautiful eyes, he tells me he was sorry for startling me and I was like no its ok I was just in my own little world and didn't pa attention to know one coming behind me. He says I will teach you words of wisdom that will take that fear away from you, he looks at me and says to me, your so beautiful my sweet little princess, how did you ever make it threw all you have been threw being as naive as you are, I know that your a lot smarter then you let on and behind that shy smile there is a very strong woman. My answer to him was "I am strong I just don't let people know so this way I wont get hurt as much". he looks at me and smiles as he says, well you are doing it all in the wrong ways, you need to show your strength so people know they cant get one by you if they had a thought of taken advantage of you they may think twice and this would avoid you even having to go threw any pain at all. I noticed he was a very wise man, and he seemed full of wisdom I could just feel it inside. He asked me how the baby was and if I needed anything, I said well the baby is great he moves so much I cant sleep much at night and I was so tired today I didn't realize I had slept my day away and that now I was wide awake, then I had told him I was sorry for sleeping so long, he didn't let me finish when he reaches his arm around my shoulders and says to me "my child you never have to say your sorry to me" this is your home if you wish it to be it's a choice you will make after we are threw talking, I am like a stranger to you but to me you're my Little girl that I have kept tabs on your life or most parts, I understand your fear and confusion but keep this in mind as a starter ok. That fear means FALSE EXPECTATIONS APPEARING REAL. I had this confused look on my face that made him laugh and he says you will understand all this real soon. He says to me are you tired, I said no, he said I want to show you something, he takes me to his office I sit down in this chair I was in this morning that was so comfortable it was like a love seat it was so big 3 or even 4 people could sit in it. He grabs this album and walks towards me and sits right next to me as he hands it to me and says I will walk you threw this. I open the album to see a little girl playing in the yard in France it was me, and me again going to school, me again dancing in the yard with this biggest smile on my face, I looked so happy I didn't even remember those days. As I looked threw the book it was nothing but pictures of me from year to year

I was growing up. There were laps between a few years here and there and he had told me he wasn't around during those times where I see a laps, because he was on a mission and couldn't be here. The laps would be between 1 to 2 years but never to far apart, I was amazed at all these pictures he had of me. I looked up at him with a smile and he puts his arm around my shoulders and gives me a kiss on the forehead as he whispers to me, "Welcome home princess"

I was getting to know the guys and Tony as the days went by and then during dinner one night as we are laughing and enjoying being together my water breaks, I was going to have my baby. Tony gets up and starts ordering everyone around to get the car and call the hospital and get my stuff, I just sat there in shock and kind of scared, "I was going to have a baby".

I made it to the hospital and the whole time driving there Tony tells me it was going to be ok and he wasn't going to leave my side, he was holding my hand and helping me breathe while my brother drove and the others stayed behind. I was taken to a room right away and checked when the doctor said I was ready to have this baby. Tony was getting ready to leave when I asked him to stay close because I would need him. He reassured me that he wasn't going anywhere's and he would be right out side the door. It went pretty fast that the minute I had my son Tony was in the room holding him, he wasn't even cleaned yet and I hadn't even had time to see him but all I could hear was "What a beautiful little man you are" in a tone of voice Tony took when he spoke with that soft voice. I see him look at me with a smile then he hands me my son, I had tears in my eyes and at that moment I was so happy, felt so safe and and didn't need drugs to feel that good, what a concept huh... But it was at that time the best moment of my life and I had a feeling that much more of these feelings were to come.

I finally get to go home with Tony and I was relieved that I had somewhere to go with someone that really cared, and a beautiful baby boy that I wasn't going to let anyone take from me. We get to the house and the guys are there all excited to see the baby and there new little guy.

The next few weeks go by fast, I spend a lot of time with the baby and learning little by little about my new family's life. Tony would spend a lot of time with me explaining to me about right from wrong and how to not allow people to fog my judgment, he would give me words of wisdom almost everyday and I listened to every word he would tell me. The guys were there on and off like they worked doing something I still hadn't figured out but didn't ask to many questions yet, I was studying all there in and outs and how they conducted themselves around Tony and how he would be with them, it was almost as if they had a secret but I hadn't figured it out, one of the guys Rick would get to go as much as the others he hung around the house and did odd things here and there to make sure there were no intruders on the property and always kept binoculars handy as well as a gun I seen stashed in the back of his pants, I didn't ask questions but instead I would watch and learn about each and every one of them until I was sure of everything. I did start to feel the safety of Tony and 2 of the brothers but the other 2 I was still in doubt of and didn't understand there weird schedule they had for like night hours. A Few months pass and my son is smiling and grabbing the attention of Tony almost every minute he was there, the brothers would always make sure they would acknowledge he was there and all the progress he was doing. Tony had a nick name for my son which was "little man" every time he would hold him he would say hey little man or when he talked about him to the brothers or myself would say "how's little man doing" I thought it was quite cute. I only wished that my oldest son and my daughter were there to spend these moments with us all. I tried to contact my ex but he had cut off all communication from me and my children and that was because he didn't even have my children it was my x father-in-law and his wife's who had my children. It was going to be tough to get them back but I wasn't about to stop trying, I knew in my heart that I will get my children back.

My baby is now almost 6 months old and my father says to me one morning " it's time you and I have a talk" I looked at him to see if I could figure out his facial features to see if it was about something I did wrong or was he going to tell me I had to leave now? I simply looked at him with a smile and said sure "when", he said to me after breakfast will be fine.

We all ate breakfast and as always I cleaned the kitchen while the guys went out to start there Harleys and would either clean them or leave for town, all I knew is that they made so much noise but they sure were one beautiful piece of machine and I was growing accustom to likening them. Once the kitchen was cleaned and I had the baby down for his nap I walked out to the front porch and my father knew by my look that I was ready to hear what he had to say to me. He gave me a motion with his hand that he would be in the house in just a moment. I made us coffee and watched out the window as he told 2 of the guys to go to town and the other 2 to stay, then they walked towards the house, I stood there looking at them as they walked in and Johnny as always had a smile on his face saying "relax your not in trouble" Tony also had that smirk on his face saying "unless you did something I don't know about" then they all laughed. I didn't know what to expect so I just smiled and I just wanted to get this over with to see what he wanted to talk to me about. I bring out coffee and give Tony a cup the other 2 said they didn't want any and I poured myself a cup, once we were all settled at the table Tony says, " ok princess the boys and I have been talking and I believe that you need to do some training on self esteem skills as well as other skills that will allow you to be stronger and better willing to face this would out here," I had this puzzled look on my face but I totally understood exactly what he was saying. He continues to say to me, I know this may be a little hard for you to take in right now but you have been used, taken advantage of, hurt in more ways I wish to express and you need to start standing up for yourself and stop letting others tell you what to do or how to run your life. I had a little smile on my face that carried happiness and a little fear because he was so right but I was still afraid to learn so I ask,

"What am I going to have to do and will I get hurt and will I be able to do this" " I mean I have been this way all my life and I'm not sure I can be tuff like you guys or for that matter stand for myself when another would be bigger or stronger or even frightening to me?" the boys started in saying they were going to have a schedule from Tony and we will take so many hours out of the day to train and teach me a whole new world. Tony then stepped in and said to me " basically I'm going to teach you how to talk like a guy, walk like a guy, fight like a guy and cheat, steal, manipulate and lie like any person that's tuff but your never going to lose the lady look and style." he also says to me "I will teach you all of this for your own good to survive in this world out here but I never want you to use it to hurt anyone or give yourself a bad reputation or cause trouble. This will be tools you keep for yourself so that never again you are afraid to stand for yourself or even fight if that is what it had to come down too, but most of all your self esteem will get a dose of hardness because lord knows your in great need. I just sat there and then I started asking questions because I was not seeing the picture Tony was drawing for me I was seeing "YES" im going to be one tuff cookie.

My training started right after I fed the baby at 6 am sharp, Tony made it to where there was a sitter for my son for the next 4 hours a day, it was this elder lady from this hotel I used to stay at off 99 she loved my son, so I was focused and could learn how to start training. I wasn't to sure of this but I was going to give it my best shot.

My training started with excurses then kick boxing followed by hitting this huge round bag, Tony was there and so was Johnny and lee to assist. I was so tired the first day I didn't know if I was going to make it back to the house, the training was no slack and I would sweat like a dog but I didn't want them to think I was afraid so I did as I was told but that last hour I was slowing down thinking all I wanted was that hot bath and to just relax in it for hours. I would listen to all the words of wisdom Tony would say to me and the boy's would show me weak points in a persons body and mind, there was so much to learn I didn't even know if I would remember all this by the next morning but I didn't lead on at all any fear or thought that I might not remember what I have learned just on the first day. This went on for weeks and I could feel myself starting to get stronger and learning right from wrong in this world of madness, there were times when things got to push and shove between me and the guy's but only to toughen me up. From doing the workout to sitting there listening to Tony talk to me about manipulating and lying to get your way without hurting people, learning to have the guts to steal something not for the rush but to feel the shame or glory, Tony would keep me for 2 hours after every workout teaching me how to stand for myself in words, how to manipulate the ones who thought they were good and to get the ones who didn't know better. He made it clear to never use all this he was teaching me to be mean or hurt anyone he was simply teaching me the ways of life in the streets and in life its self, but I was feeling it get to my head and started to think I was all that ands then some, I hide it well but knew I could do this with no problem.

After 6 months of hard work and training and listening to all the words of wisdom I could take I thought I was one of the guys, I would fight them to see if I could win, I would manipulate them to see if I got away with it and at some point I did, to there disappointment in themselves, I was getting good at all I was being taught and I was loving every minute of it. Then came time to learn how to hold a gun and use a gun as well as the knife and any tool that came to hand. This part for me was hard because I was never a weapon person but I was willing to learn everything I was being taught, this was starting to be addictive and I was getting off on learning all this stuff. By the time I hit 10 months with all this knowledge I was like one of the guys, I walked like a guy talked like a guy and acted tuff like a guy, it was my sense of shield I guess but it felt good to me, I knew deep inside I wasn't going to ever again let someone hurt me. Tony was noticing the difference in me but in a worried way so he sat me down and says to me "your a woman not a man and you need to keep your priorities in perspective this fear you feel you need to conquer isn't what I wanted to teach you, what I want you to know is that FEAR means False Expectations Appearing Real', so the choice was mine to figure out, he was good at things like this, explaining the goodness out of words I didn't care for or would even admit, but he always saw right threw me and seemed to fix any kind of denial I had or any misunderstanding of words I needed to apply to my life.

I got to see he was a good man, one of principles but good threw his heart, he made it clear when he was serious and wanted something but then again he had a heart of gold and would of gave you anything you wanted. He was very bright and knew exactly what he needed to do to get what ever it was he wanted, he seemed to just have that way about his self. He was a charmer but then again to smart to just charm anyone. The next few weeks go by fast, I spend a lot of time with the baby and learning little by little about my new family's life. Tony would spend a lot of time with me explaining to me about right from wrong and how to not to believe everything that I hear, One night after dinner he says to me, "meet me in my office when the little man is sleeping". After a few hours I walked to his office and he asked me to close the door, he seemed serious so I did as I was told. He asked me to sit down so he could talk to me, I did and he proceeds to let me know he had to go away for a little while, he told me he was a navy seal and worked for the government and he wouldn't be back for at least 3 months but he promised me he would return, I didn't understand so I asked him "why" but he says to me "you ask to many questions and I will answer them as we go and to the best of my ability but there are some things you just can't know, this is one of them" just know that I have work to do and you will be safe here with the boy's, he explained to me he was taking Lee with him and that Jake would be in charge of watching the property for safety, Michael was in charge of watching the house and Johnny would be in the house with me and the baby, he continued to let me know that he had hired a few other men to watch outside the gates so I had nothing to be afraid of and that we would be safe. I had this puzzled look on my face as I listened then I had to ask, why all the security were we in some kind of danger. His look was soft then he just smiled saying, not only do I work for the government but I am a hell's angel which means there are some bad people out there and he wanted to just make sure I and the baby was safe when he wasn't around. I then asked him if this hell's angel was the group he rode motorcycles with. He decided to educate me on biker's and what they mean and don't mean, what stuck in my head the most after a hour of him explaining what a motorcycle "gang" was and what it represented was the last words he said about it, he looked at me hoping I had understood all he had just spoke to me about and finished with, "The Biker is the 'no' to the great American 'yes' which is stamped so big over our official culture But, as we know, biker, hell angel's movies never end happily. Right?".

All I knew was Tony and his son's always rode these beautiful huge motorcycles, they would meet up with another dozen riders and they would go for hour long rides, they all had tattoo's all over and they wore these scarf's blue or red on there heads tied in the back, never hardly wearing helmets, they were loud bikes and the men were roudy by the time they came back but they would always end up in the guest house about 500 feet from the main house, a place I was told to never go to, that it was the men's house to meet and work together, and as always I did as I was told so I actually had never even been in there.

As I was day dreaming Tony interrupts by saying, when I return I will teach you how to ride as a passenger then how to ride on your own. At first it seemed scary to me but I wanted to be a part of them so I was willing to do whatever it took. He asked me if I had any questions about him leaving. When I said no he right away says to me "now here are the dos and don'ts and I expect you to abide by them to your fullest respect of this family. I looked at him with a very honest smile and nods. He proceeds to tell me that I wasn't to leave this property alone, that I wasn't to bring anyone home and that he expected me to actually stay put and have Johnny or one of the other brothers go get me anything I needed. He continued to let me know that there were things he did that was important and sometimes not so good and that this was simply for my own safety, I didn't want to pry or ask so many questions but I felt close enough to him now to ask probing questions and want a answer, doing it all with respect and as much grace as I could. I was finding that Tony's little girl could get away with that, actually Tony's little girl was getting away with a lot of things, I just didn't flaunt It or try to let my his son's be to aware of it, not just yet anyways.

The next morning I woke up and I knew he was gone. And I was walking towards Tony's office when I seen J in there and he was doing drugs. I could see the white powder on the mirror and him getting it together to snort or smoke it. He looks up to see I was there watching and he smiles at me as he says you want some. I walked towards him and said yes. From that point on I was doomed because I knew it was on and I wasn't going to stop.

We did drugs for like a week and it was so bad that we decided to leave there and go to Santa Cruz CA. where know one can find us or see us this way we wouldn't get into trouble. "So we thought" So I pack up some of my stuff and my son and off I go to California with j. First place we arrive at was Santa Cruz flats where you find all the drugs. We got ourselves a hotel room and it was on. After about 2 weeks there doing what we did I had told j that Tony was coming but he thought I was just tweaking. I knew better and for some reason I knew he was going to show up it was like in my skin but I just knew he was going to be there real soon. It wasn't 1 hour there he was pounding in the front door of the hotel room angry as angry can be. He had this look on his face I would never forget but he never said word to me, he looked at me with a look that simply killed me and he right away went to make sure my son was ok then he attacks j saying this was all his fault and to get out. He kicked out j and made me sit in that room till he was done with business. I knew I was in for it but I was as well high so it didn't matter to me much I just wanted to sleep for a few hours. It was Christmas Eve and I had no Christmas tree for my son or any presents because my drugs came first and it's what I made my priority each and every day.

Tony had got some food and fed my son and myself and it was getting late but he wanted to talk to me and he loved the ocean so he said to me, "let's go to the beach and have a walk we need to talk"

We were walking on the beach and he was talking to me about getting help, telling me that this was no way of life that he didn't teach me all this stuff the last few years for me to turn out this way, I heard what he was saying but all I had in my head was where I was going to get my next fix because I was starting to withdraw from the drugs. My son was holding his hand and he had his arm around my shoulders, I heard a fight about 200 feet away from us and I was looking to see what it was and what was going on, Tony seen me look and said to pay no mind to them and to listen to what he was trying to tell me but I kept trying to look. It was a gang of Mexicans engaging into a huge fight. Tony turns me away from looking as he continued to try to talk sense to me about getting help when I hear like 4 to 5 different shots from a gun and when I turned to see where it came from or who was shooting who I seen Tony fall to his knee's and face first into the sand. A bullet and gone our way by accident and went through Tony's back and to his heart which Killed him instantly. I remember that I fell to my knees and grabbed him yelling and crying out his name, I turned him over onto my lap and I was screaming, my son was crying also but I didn't even pay attention to him all I could do is hold Tony in my arms he was bleeding and was dead in my arms.

The sound of ambulances and fire trucks drove me nuts, the sirens were so loud I couldn't take it, it got to the point where I couldn't even hear my son screaming, I was crying so loud, I remember seeing the gang run and the cops walking towards me in the sand. I was crying my son was crying the sirens were so loud it drove me nuts, I remember me asking them to turn them off, please turn them off. The police was approaching me but I wasn't about to let them take Tony away from me so I put my hand in his vest and said he had a gun and if anyone came any closer to take him away I was going to shoot them. There was police all over, firefighters and ambulances I didn't hear the police come up behind me and grabbed my son and then they tried to talk me into giving up the gun and letting the paramedics take Tony. What they didn't know was there was no gun under his vest I just didn't want them to take him away from me.

I was crushed, I just lost my everything, Tony, my best friend, A Father I never had, my GOD and I wasn't ready to let him go yet. I was still crying and didn't even pay attention to what they had done and took my son I just didn't and couldn't believe what had just happened. My world was crushed. There was a police officer who tried to get closer to talk to me , he had asked me to please had him the gun under that vest and to let the ambulance take Tony away, he was making promises to me and I was still crying, I was so devastated that I was confused not understanding what had just happened, how within seconds my whole world was crushed and I wanted to just die.

The police finally got close enough to realize that there was never a gun, they grabbed me and the paramedics took Tony away, I was put into a police car and taken to town. I was being questioned about what had just happened, what I saw and heard and how all this came about. All I could think of is that it was all my fault, if I would of never disrespected Tony by getting high we would of never been on that beach at that time and he would still be here. I was so dead inside so numb and wanted to simply die, I didn't care no more what happened to me, I was now so tired, crying still, getting so sleepy and withdrawing from drugs. The police told me they took my son and he was going to be sent to family while I figured out what I was going to do with my life, I so didn't care and it's like I didn't even hear them, everything was like a eco.

I finally got released from jail I remember there were 2 police officers who really cared and wanted to help me but at that point I didn't care, I just wanted out of there, I walked out of the jail after 6 months and crying and just not caring about nothing no more. I found myself walking the street when I ran upon 2 hookers who had a hotel room not far, they knew who I was everyone by that time had heard about the gang shooting and the man on the beach getting hit by accident. They seen I was so out of it that they took me by the arm and took me to there room. As I sat there they spoke to me saying not to worry they will take care of me for the time being. I started to cry again when one of them said to me "im going to give you something that will help you with the pain and make you feel better" they came towards me with a needle that had brown stuff in it, I didn't care just take this pain away from me and they did. They injected me with what you call a speedball which was a mixture of cocaine and heroin.

It took like 30 seconds and I felt this mixture go through my veins, within another 10 seconds I felt the best high I ever had, there was no more pain I was feeling, no more crying, it took away every fiber within me of fear, hopelessness, pain and I felt like know one could hurt me again, I felt strong and ready to face the world in a all new way.

From that point on it was like I did anything to never let this feeling leave my body, this meant I had to stay high like this 24/7 and I did. The 2 hookers taught me how to sell my soul, how to cheat, manipulate and steal. For the next 7 months I did just that and I stayed high 24/7 with that heroin which became my best friend. I had know one left my kids were all gone Tony was gone and I was left alone. My family has disowned me because of the drugs ad all my bad choices. I didn't fear nothing that came near me no matter if it was a 200 pound man or woman or if it was a handful of people I didn't care, I was on a roll, I felt no pain, no sorrow, no guilt or pity I felt simply nothing and I liked feeling this way and wasn't bout to change. This was my new way of life and I loved every minute of it.

I was selling my soul to get that next hit no matter what I had to do for it and had no regrets about how I did it. I was so high I just didn't care, There was one time when I had gotten a bag of heroin from these twins they were Mexican and before I left to go do it I realized they had sold me some fake stuff, I was mad and started to argue with them in the middle of the street, I could see the hookers on one side of the street and other drug dealers on the other, by that time everyone knew who Frankie was and most kept there distant because they thought I was a nut case and they all knew that I was a bottle of anger waiting to explode. As I argued with these twins I hit one of them and the other came at me, I started to fight them both with not a fiber of fear within me, I could her on one side of the streets the hookers cheering me on and the other side the dealers cheering me on, the more I heard the cheers the more I got into fighting these 2 boys, I had kicked the crap out of them and took there dope, as I was walking away from them I seen this small woman about 4 feet tall and weighed like 200 pounds coming towards me, I thought I was all that and showing off in front of everyone watching I would say to her as she approached me " come on bitch, you want a piece of me too?" and the closer she got to me the more I realized it was the mother of the twins I just fought and stole there dope but that didn't scare me, I stood there waiting for her to get closer and was ready to kick her ass too until she took a swing at me caught me off guard and knocked me down, once I was down she started to kick the crap out of me to where I couldn't even defend myself and she got the better of me until the hookers started to come my way and the woman left. Once again I was being rescued by the hookers, they were girlfriends to each other aka lesbians and they seemed to leave people alone and minded there own, but they were also great friends to me, they never tried to get me to do anything with them and they seemed to just like me as there friend I guess because they always seemed to come to my rescue just at the right time. I didn't care all I knew is that they were nice to me or were they just scared? Either way I didn't care for I felt nothing so it didn't matter to me.

I now had my own hotel room and I did what I had to do to get my dope, I would go into stores and fill a cart full of clothes then go out the back door, I would then put them into bags and walked out like I had just bought everything, never being noticed. I would take the stolen clothes to the dope mans house and he would trade me dope for the items. This went on for a while until I got caught and I ran out of that store and kept running until they lost me. Now I had to think of new scam to get my drugs.

I had gone over to the hookers hotel room to see if they had some drugs to help me out and as always they did, they were doing a 3 some with some guy and didn't seem to let me bother them sense they answered the door half naked and told me to go to the kitchen and get my fix that they would be right there so I did. I was in that kitchen and I could her them I was like damn when are they going to finish so I could get the hell out. I couldn't just leave because I would have to go through the bedroom to get to the door and he was in the bathroom when they let me in but once I was in the kitchen they were all three in the bedroom so that meant I had to wait until they were done before I could go out. I fixed my habit with cocaine and heroin and sat there enjoying my high but had to hear them three in that bedroom I wanted to go, I was never one to sit still, I was always on the go. So I decided to go out the window, this way I wouldn't bother them and I could go on with my high and all. I remember once I was out the window and on my way down the road I could see the girls laughing because I wouldn't sit in there and wait until they were done. They knew me so well, I was the kind of girl that was always on the go, never to sit still or longer then I had too.

Running the streets I was treating my adduction as a crime or moral deficiency, I became rebellious and was driven deeper into isolation. Some of my high's felt great but eventually the things I had to do to continue using reflected desperation, I was so caught in the grip of my addiction, I had to have drugs at all cost. Failure and fear began to invade my life which lead me my inability to deal with life on life's terms. It was a very hostile world out there and I would try to justify my right to use, it worked for a while but then I was right back to the same old thing, feeling that worthlessness deep down inside which indicted that there was something wrong with me, or that know one was left to love me so why not. My character defects were so familiar to me by now and knew exactly what I was doing or about to do, the sad part about it was that know one cared and I felt so alone so using my drugs made me feel like I was important or that people places or things liked me, I felt strong and full of life thinking that this was going to be my life for the rest of my life.

I remember there was this lady who was older like about 70 and she used drugs very strongly, when she got high she would tell stories and I would go over to see her and listen for hours as I cleaned for her and cooked her dinner, she had bad legs always very swollen and she couldn't get around very well so I knew that every time I went there she was always happy to see me because she knew I would clean and cook for her and of course in exchange I would get drugs from her.

She would ask me, "do you know who God is?, I would answer well of course, she would say when do you talk to God?, I would say, when im on my way to the dope mans house and I would ask God, "please let him be home" or when I see cops I would ask God "please don't let me get busted" and I would laugh after I would say that. She would look at me and say shame on you. She would tell me, " your ability to talk to God is an important part of your life" she would say "you need to communicate with him in a way that shows your humility and invites his intervention." I looked at her and would say, "now how do you expect me to talk to God when im high?. Or knowingly know that what im doing is wrong?" "there's no way im going to talk to God, he has taken away everything I loved in my life, he has put me through bad trips as a kid and a young adult, he has made it to where people hurt me and abused me". she would take a smoke off her pipe then rest her head on the back of her chair then she would look at me and say, "so you think all that was Gods fault?" I looked at her with a sad voice and answered, Yes". she looked at me and said, "the choices I have made to use drugs are all mine and mine alone, the wrongs I have done are all mine also, God had nothing to do with my wrong choices but he still loves me". "I 'm just waiting to die and be with him to ask for forgiveness knowing he will". she continues to say to me, "I have nothing to live for anymore and if I stop doing drugs now it will kill me and I know this so I just keep using knowing that soon it will be my time to be with him and I will be forgiven". I'm thinking well its not all that easy and I am to ashamed to even talk to god about anything right now, I'm angry at him for giving me a life of hell and nothing will change that. I was convinced that I must have done something really bad in my past life to have been given the life I had. Anyways I would tell her, "Come on tell me a story Betty and enough about this God stuff". She would smile and say "one day you will pray and for all the right reasons and know God will be there unconditionally for you." Anyways she would start telling me stories of when she was married and hadn't done drugs yet how happy she was and how her daughter was her life, ect ect. I liked to listen to her because it made me dream the undreamable, wishing I had that love or that closeness with someone in my family or even my children. Never thinking that I had created this wall between me and anyone that loved me. I would listen to betty until I had enough then I would go, I knew she had her clean house and her diner so it was time for me to go, I never stayed in one spot to long. I knew Betty loved me because she always held my hand every time I left and would say to me "God bless you my sweet child". Know I love you". "I would hug her and say, see you in a couple days Betty". Every time I left her house I was not only high as a kite but I felt good knowing she really really liked me for just me and nothing else.

Someone Cared

It was about 11 pm July 3ed 1995, my 7 month run sense Tony died was getting to an end. I was walking the streets, hadn't used sense that morning because I didn't have money to get drugs and couldn't find anyone home or around to give me any, I was cold had no place to go, lost my room I had because I had no money and I was starting to have withdrawals and knew I needed a fix real quick. I stood against a cement wall in a corner of a road just starting to cry, feeling lost and not knowing what was going to happen to me, as I stood there a black car pulls up and stops, the door on the passenger side opens and a man who was about 60 or more bends over the seat and says get in. My first thought was gaud now what, and as a dumb ass I get in the car. As the man starts driving I ask him do you have drugs. He looked at me and reaches in his vest pocket and pulls out a badge and puts it in my face. I thought God now im going to jail and I need a fix bad. The man stops the car and starts to tell me, I am a judge for drug court, my daughter killed herself out here with drugs and Tony was my best friend, I have been looking for you for a while now and I will NOT let you destroy your life any longer out here or will I read in the paper about you dieing of a over dose. He proceeds to tell me that I have a ton of charges pending on me at this time and if I allowed him to help me he would make sure that the charges would go away little by little. He continued to talk to me about Tony and his daughter, it was a sad story but I didn't care I was withdrawing I was tired I wanted to lay down and sleep I wanted to eat then I would go about my business. All I could think of was God im so withdrawing and this dude is trying to talk nonsense that I don't even want to hear. He continues to drive until we get to this hospital and he says to me, "you will go here to detox and

I will come back to get you to take you somewhere safe. I had know where's to go and I was so tired all I wanted to do was sleep. He told me if I stayed there for a week to detox he would take a charge away for me, my charges were, possession, intent to sell, distribution, failure to appear, running from the police, and the list went on and on. I didn't even care at that time all I wanted was a bed and a worm place to sleep so I told him ok.

A week later just as I was feeling good I didn't like it, I was starting to feel and all these bad feelings I had were coming back, the death of Tony and all the stuff that had happened to me as a child I didn't want to see but it was there in my head, I thought I have to leave this place and get high this way I wont feel all this and be numb again but it was well wishing because at that same moment the judge came in and said " are you ready?" I looked at him ad said "ready for what?" he says to me " ready for your next journey, I'm taking you to a rehab where there are other people, it's a co-ed rehab and you get to leave during the day to find a job, you pay your way, they feed you and house you, you have to do meetings which are Narcotic anomious meetings, you will have to get up in the morning and be gone by 9 am and be back by 5 pm to eat diner then you start working a program that consists of you working steps which they will explain to you all that you will be doing. This program is a 6 month program and if you complete this then you will be free of all charges and hopefully be ready to start a new life". I am thinking well heck they let you leave during the day wow that's easy I can do that I will get high during the day and come back and do my program, plus it was co-ed?…heck yea that sounded real easy so I tell him "ok sure im ready" he had a smile on his face but it was like a smile of "yea we'll see".

The ride to the rehab was pretty quiet, he had asked me a few questions like "so are you feeling better?" and I would say as good as expected I guess then he started to tell me about how he knew Tony and talked about his daughter and how he wished he did for here what he was about to do for me. Al I knew was that lets just get there so I can get cut loose and go get high, that's all I had in my head and was getting so excited about the thought of getting high again. We arrive at the rehab it was called New life comminute services. I walk in with judge T and

I see people outside smoking cigarettes and people just sitting inside chilling. I'm thinking hum so far so good, judge T tells me to sit at a table and he will go in the office to have me in rolled. As I sat there I was wanting a cigarette real bad, I had nothing but the clothes on my back, no money no ciggs nothing, I was thinking oh joy this is going to be fun with a sarcastic thought. So I walk out to smoke I bum a smoke from this guy sitting there and as I was starting to smoke I got a head rush because I hadn't had a cigarette in a week and I was smoking it to fast but that head rush felt so good I could hardly wait to get to leave this place to get high. I get called in the office and the judge says to me, "good luck, I will come by to check on you" I looked at him and said ok and he walked away.

I'm in the office and they start to tell me im on a 2 week contract meaning I cant leave my first 2 weeks and I have to be with a pear buddy at all times, they proceed to tell me that they drug test any time they want and that I was to behave and be at my best behavior wile I was there. My heart started to sink, I'm thinking oh my god now im stuck here for another 2 weeks and have to listen to all this crap there saying I have to do, I was assigned a chore to do which was bathrooms and I was to have it done by 10 am, then they proceeded to tell me that the judge had left money on my books so I could get shampoo, toothpaste and cigarettes and ect. But they wasn't going to let me go to the store I was to make a list of what I wanted and they would make sure I had it by the end of that day. I'm thinking this rely sucks and why did I agree to all this again? God I figured ok 2 more weeks I can do this hell I did it a week so might as well wait another 2 weeks before I could get high again, regardless that I was wanting it so bad NOW but I wasn't withdrawing no more so I could wait 2 more weeks. I was taken to my room which was a room with 2 other girls in it, I was given a set of sheets, blankets, pillows and hangers, then they took me to this other room where they had clothes that were donated and they tell me to pick anything I wanted and needed so I could have clothes for myself, so I got me lots of clothes and that was about the excitement of my day. Then they assigned me a peer buddy whom was another client there that had been there for like 5 months and was about to graduate from there soon so she knew the ropes of everything, she walks up to me and says come on lets go outside and I can

Explain to you all the rules and regulations and I will give u some cigarettes until you get yours. I was thinking wow there is a god; I can finally have a full smoke. I sat there for like 2 hours with her as she went over all the do's and don'ts and it was about that time that everyone had to be back so I would see guys and gals coming in from where ever they came from, I am thinking hum there are some cute guys in here. Maybe I can make these next 2 weeks a fun 2 weeks what the heck right?.

Dinner was served and right after that we had like a ½ hour until meetings would start. First meeting was just the women with counselor's for an hour, then we had what they call aftercare meeting which was everyone who lived at the facility that lasted a hour and then was the NA meeting where people from all over that was in recovery would come to for an hour. It was different for me and I felt a little out of place because not only was I clean from drugs for a week but I was starting to feel and I wasn't liking how I was feeling. I sat through the meeting and the person speaking was talking about death, I couldn't handle it no more, I couldn't sit there and listen to what this speaker was talking about when I had just lost Tony and these feelings were so real it was killing me. I got up from the meeting and went outside, it was dark and I had tears in my eyes, I look up to the sky thinking "are you really for real God?" then I say out loud as I'm crying thinking I'm all alone "why God?, why did you take away from me the nicest person in my life, the most caring and the only man I looked up too that really taught me to be who I am, why did you give me this life and why are you making me so miserable, what did I ever do to deserve all this crap!!!"

Then all the sudden I heard a voice out of know where's that says to me "and what makes you so damn special" I turn around to see a shadow sitting on the bench and it was this woman who I had met earlier as a counselor. Needless to say the thought in my head was "bitch" but I didn't say it I just looked at her. She stood up and said we needed to talk but after the meeting and that I was to get my butt back in there for now. Without a word I went back in to the meeting and sat there, I couldn't even hear what the speaker was saying I was just looking all around me thinking that there was now way that al these people were clean from drugs, there was just no way. The meeting ended and I went right to my room and went to bed, I didn't want to talk to that counselor nor anyone else.

I wake up the next morning to noise being made by the girls I shared the room with they were getting ready to go to work, I got up not saying a word and slipped on some sweats and went out side hoping that someone would give me a cigarette. As I was walking out side one of the staff members waves me to go to the office so I do and they tell me that my peer buddy will go with me to the store today to get things I need, that money was left on my books for me to get whatever I needed and that I was allowed to keep the rest of the money on me if I wanted. All I did was nod my head and went back towards the door to go out side because I wanted that cigarette really bad. Of course to everyone I was a new comer is what they called people like me who was new to the program, but I had so much anger in me I wasn't about to be some soft female that was going to be told what to do or be pushed around, if there was going to be any pushing around to be done it was going to be me to them period. I had and have been through so much in my life and especially the last year that I wasn't about to give anyone the pleasure to see me cry or have there way with me, I was done and wasn't afraid to say it or show it.

I sat there smoking and people were coming and going I felt like I was in a damn jungle and nosey, God they would see me and say hi what's your name and how long are you hear for, did you go to jail did you get court ordered blah, I just looked at them and said "why don't you just mind your own business and let me take care of my own and we will do just fine" some thought it was amusing others just looked at me and didn't say a word. I mean your talking about a girl who has been brought to a strange place where I knew know one, had so much anger in me I was about to crack and was so confused that if someone said something that wasn't exactly good to say I might of bit there head off, I had tattoos on my for arms on the back of my neck and on my chest so that alone didn't make me look to nice and I didn't even care, I was given some cigarettes and I was happy, now leave me the hell alone.

As I was there longer I started to get a little more adjusted, I had found me a job at a near restaurant and the owner was French Canadian so she spoke French and it was nice that I could talk to her from time to time in French, she had 2 daughters and a son and they were all so nice to me, she knew I was in recovery and that I hadn't been there very long but for some reason I started to really like her and trust her, she was about 10 years older then I was but something about her I felt drawn to her and safe around her. She showed trust I me and lots of care and I appreciated her for that, it had been a long time sense I was cared for like that. I would work from 7 am at times till 10 pm all depends on how busy we were and it seemed that the more we hired people to work the more they would mess up and would have to leave so pretty much it left me and Nicole the owner to work the best we can together. She did all the cooking and I did the witnessing, her daughters would come help when they could and we had a couple good waitresses that were still there but talk about short handed, and I still had my program to work so I had to be in every night by 6 pm.

Once I returned to the program after work it was diner then get ready to have meetings until 10 pm, some days I didn't eve want to be there wanted my own place so I could come and go as I wanted but by then I knew I was in the best and safest place for the moment so I adjusted ad did as I was supposed too. The founder and owner of the program I was at "New Life Community Center" his name was Steven Styles he was a tuff cookie, he knew exactly how to approach you and how to get you to come out of your shell. He knew I had some shyness about me but he knew damn well I was as hard as a rock inside and he was bound and determined to break it up.

I found myself liking the program a lot, I felt safe there and knew for a fact that I wasn't going to use as long as I stayed there. I was starting to gain my self confidence again and realizing that I was a pretty good person, a lot better then I ever thought through out my whole life. I was feeling really good and knew it was time to start working on getting my kids back I knew it was going to be a struggle but I was ready to face whatever it took to do it.

I would never miss work, I was prompt to my meetings and participated in whatever I had to so I could be respected and seen for who I really was, I had a sponsor whom was the best thing I ever did, she was good to me but didn't let nothing pass by if she thought I was trying to over do myself or try to pull one past her, she told me like it was but then again she had heart and greatness about her that I had ever seen in my life. She decided it was time to face my past and all my fears, things I was angry about but didn't know exactly what, things I had blocked off in my head and couldn't pin point so my sponsor asked me if I was willing to get hypnotized and she would tape it and it would stay completely confidential and we would work from there to complete my dark anger I had blocked out in my life. I was scared but I agreed because no matter how bad it was going to be I needed to get through it and over it, so we scheduled it for that following week on a Friday morning and I would spend the weekend with my sponsor in case I needed support or needed her just because.

I think that was one of the longest weeks in my life, everyday I would think about getting hypnotized and tried to remember stuff but couldn't and was worried about, what could I have done that was so bad that I had blocked it out of my head and life?. Or what was so bad that something had maybe happened to me and didt want to face it ad that was why I had blocked it, I didn't know but all I knew is that I had to get through this so I could continue on in my life with no more monsters or fears I felt so deep down inside and wondered if that was the reason of my anger towards people was or if tht was the reason I started to use drugs or if that was the reason that I felt I needed to always be a part of or do bad things, I didn't know but I did want to know so all that week I tortured myself in trying to justify all my wrongs on "what", "why", and "how". I didt tell kowonne about my rondevous with a hipnosis with my sponsor, as far as anyone knew I was just going to spend the weekend with my sponsor and work some steps.

That Friday came and I was so scared, I told my sponsor I was scared and she had told me that it was ok, that she expected me to be scared nd if I wasn't then she would call it a problem. She would tell me " your right where your supposed to be" I hated it whe she would say that but I knew she was right. She picked me up at 8 am from the program, I had what you call a weekend pass and I had gotten the weekend off from work. She assured me it was going to be ok and she was going to be there all the wy with me. I trusted her with all my heart, we had formed a bond of loyality, trust and friendship that I never had ever with a woman, she was like a mother figure as well as a best friend and would always tell me, "I love you unconditionally" no matter what you did in your past or what was done to you I will never let you down and always be there for you. She was so sweet and wonderful, she has 15 years more clean time then I had and she knew that NA book from front to back almost by heart, her husband was ill but he was so nice and supported her recovery 100 percent, during our ride to get hypnotized she would tell me that from now on I will have to learn how to put recovery first In my life along with God, she had told me that after this weekend I will have a total different outlook on myself and my life and she would hope that I will find the answers to all my "why's" and move on with my life. She also made sure to tell me that no matter what happened that I needed to have forgiveness in my heart and know that no matter what, "people, places and things" have changed in life and I needed to keep that I mind. Almost like she already knew what I was going to say under hypnoses and hoped I would forgive whoever or maybe myself, I didn't know, all I knew is that I was really scared for some reason but I also knew I needed to know I just needed to know.

We arrived at this house, it was big and so beautiful, my sponsor grabs my arm and says to me, "come on it's going to be ok" she rings the door bell and this lady comes to the door and hugs my sponsor and gives me a hug as well when my sponsor introduces me. We go ito the house it was so nice, the lady takes us to a room it was like a office and she gets us ice tea and cokes, and coffee, has everything set up for us and it was a very safe looking environment. The lady proceeds to explain what was going to happen and how she was going to hypnotize me, she made me feel real comfortable and assured me I was going to be ok, if she felt I was going to get to upset or anything wrong that she would stop. I listened to everything she was telling me and made sure I understood everything and asked any question I felt I needed to ask. My sponsor assured me I was going to be ok ad that she was going to be there the whole time with me. This was going to take all day if needed but I was about to get rid of all my ghosts and fears I had deep down inside and I had blocked out for some reason not knowing why but I was ready.

We sat and spoke for a while so I would feel at ease I had some Tea and was ready. My sponsor gives me a hug and says to me, "remember! "unconditionally". she was so nice, and her friend grabs my hand nd makes me lay down on this couch that was like a easy chare but it was a couch, I layed there got comfortable and looked her in the eyes as she started to hypnotize me. All I remember is falling asleep, seeing like colors and different things around me but not scared at all and feeling really comfortable for now.

My sponsors friend had me lay down and relax, she asked me to close my eyes and count from ten down and I did, before I knew it I was out. She spoke to me and I responded but I didn't kow what I was saying it was like I was in another world, clouded and peaceful, then she asked me to go back to when I was a little girl starting at six years old and I did. I would tell her what I was seeing and she asked me questions as I answered, I felt happiness then all the sudden fear hit me, I was in a dark place, it was so scary and I started to cry, she spoke very calmly to me and had me tell her where I was and what was happening, Gawd I could see him, he smelled of alcohol and I was so afraid, I could see myself crying and so afraid, he had a whip and he was spanking me, I was crying then he picked me up and made me sit on a table, we were outside in a shed and then he would say he was sorry and hugged me but the hug wasn't a hug of regret from his part it was a hug a child should never get. His hand would touch me in places I didn't like and I would cry, he would take my hand and make me touch him in places that I didt like, he would tell me to stop crying or I would get another spanking, I could feel the tears on my face and the fear I felt, I was so scared and confused, I didn't know what he was doing but I know I didn't like him touching me. I didn't look at him because of fear and kept my face towards the shed window. It didn't take long that he stopped touching me and he picked me up and put me to my feet telling me that I had better not say a word or I would get a beating that would make me bleed. He then took my hand and took me back towards the house where my mother was there cooking diner, I remember running to my room and hiding behind the curtains. My mother had o idea what he had done and she thought I ran to my room because I had just gotten punished for being bad ad that was why I ran to my room. We still lived in France at that time. What had just happened, I didn't know but I did know that whatever he made me touch it wasn't good or something a little girl should even have to do.

The voice makes me continue my journey under hypnoses and tells me to tell her what I was doing and seeing. I remember seeing my mother crying after my step father had hit her because he was drunk, she was packing for us to go to America. I didn't like seeing my mother cry, it made me sad, I remember reaching up to her and caressing her cheek and she had hugged me saying it was all going to be ok. I loved it when my mother hugged me, I needed her right now so bad but couldn't tell her what had happened because of the fear I had of him. I continue on to a few years past, we were in America now and I see my step dad drunk all the time, yelling at my mom I would see her cry in her room and it broke my heart, I wanted my mother so bad and couldn't go to her, he had seen me looking at her and he had that look that I feared so bad. I was about 10 at that time and I would beg my mother to ot go to work, she didn't understand why I would throw a fit and would get mad at me telling me she had to go to work. I didn't want to be left home with him, even though by then I had my brother and sisters I was still so afraid of him. For the last four years he had abused me the same way he did the first time whe I was six except now I had sisters and I wasn't about to let him get near them and hurt them. He would smell of alcohol and he would say, if you don't do it I will get your sisters. I hated him I hated his guts the bastard. I will die before I let him touch my sisters, and he would say as I got older that if I ever spoke of this he would hurt them and my mom. Him and his drunk self I wanted him to die. I was crying again and the voice calmed me down, asked me about my brothers and sisters to get me out of that pain as she knew when I spoke of them I smiled and was happy, I loved my sisters so much and my brothers, at the age of 16 I would of died for them before I ever let anyone hurt them, I would talk about how they were special to me because my mom worked so much that I spent a lot of time with them and we were very close as kids. But I couldn't help but to go back to this dark place again, I could hear the footsteps at night and I was in bed hiding under my sheets praying he wouldn't open my door. I was so scared, my sisters and brothers were sleeping in another room, ad I was afraid to be in my room alone because I knew he would come in, after all his drinking. My room was the first room in the hall then my brothers then my sisters so I knew at least they were safe but God help me I was so scared. I would wrap my sheets around me so tight and pretend I was sleeping every time I heard his foots steps come towards my door, I remember hearing the door knob turn slowly and he opened the door, I would shake and start to cry, the most quietest cry anyone ever heard. I didn't want him to see me crying, the lights were off it was dark all you could see was the lights from the hallways so he wouldn't see my face but I felt him sit on my bed and he would reach for my hand to put on him, he made me grab him and I felt his other hand touch me in places I didn't want him to touch, I was dieing inside, God please make it stop I would think to myself as I cried. Then I hear that soft voice again calming me down and making me go to another place that was good for me. I would always go back to the kids, they made me smile they were my life and I loved them so much. I continued on for about an hour then I was waked up.

I could feel the tears on my eyes so I knew I had cryed but didn't remember nothing that I had said, it was all being taped so I would hear it later. We had decided to make it a series of 4 sittings and figured that this would find my hidden anger and reasons to always want to run away or escape reality when I would have to face it, or to give me the answers as to why I mde the choices I did in my life, there had to be a reason and now I wanted to know.

My sponsor's friend came with us to my sponsor's house and she was going to stay with us that weekend so we could finish this hypnotized tapeing and I could move on with my life. We had decided to not listen to the tapes untill I was all done with my sittings and that by Sunday it would be all done. Yes I was scared but I did want to hear those tapes so us three spent a great diner together had some good laughs and talked about lots of things, positive things, the energy was great and I was feeling wonderful, I was away from the program for the weekend, I was with great company and I was safe.

I tried to call my son Aaron that weekend but his dad wouldn't let me talk to him, this wasn't the first time he did that but did my son know I even tried to call so much sense I had been in the program. I had told myself that my goals were going to be that I reunite with my children and never again will I let them stray away, "never again"

That evening we decided to work on the tapeings again, again when I woke up I was in tears, this I didn't like because I was wondering what was it that I had blocked out that was so bad that I would always cry, I would soon find out. That Saturday we did 2 more sections of hypnoses and it was all done, my sponsor let me know that it was better to wait till the morig to hear them she felt I needed to rest so I agreed, I always agreed with her because she always knew best, her words of wisdom gave me courage to keep going, her unconditional love gave me hope that I as well will be a mom again, and her friendship aside of being my sponsor gave me the faith that I would one day be as good as she was. I had been with her sense July15th, I got clean on July 4th 1995 but wet to detox and jail untill the 15th and then she became my sponsor, I didn't ask her to be she just worked her way in my life knowing I needed lots of help and patience to get through all this and stay clean. Her husband had passed not long before I came in the program; he as well had like 20 years clean before he passed but he had a heart attack and didn't make it. My sponsor was a great wonderful woman, a mother figure, a best friend and a leader in life. Her name was Jackie but we called her NA Jae because she was as tuff as tarzans Jane, to make a long story short she would call her husband Tarzan. Anyways it's Saturday night about 8 pm and we were sitting out side watching the waves from my sponsors deck and her friend Lena who Hypnotized me was also there. I at that time had like 10 months clean, I was working a 12 step program, doing my program, working and doing everything I would to get my son back from Oregon. My daughter was with my sister but we were not talking yet, I had some huge amends to make to her before we would ever reunite and my oldest son was I France so that as well was going to have to be a goal also is make amends to him and let them all kow I loved them unconditionally and that I was so so so sorry for all I had done, by making myself misurable I made them misurable, by hurting myself it hurt them as well and by doing drugs I had lost them. My heart would hurt because when you're not using drugs you "feel", you remember and you're ashamed. I had lots of work to do for my children to be back I my life, but I wasn't going to give up because I AM there mother and I DO love them with all my life andair I breathe so I had my work cut out for me in the coming year.

I looked at my sponsor and at lena and I say "I want to hear the tapes", they looked at each other then back at me as my sponsor says to me, "are you sure you wnt this Frankie, we can wait untill tomorrow but if your sure you want to do this ow then we will. I looked at my sponsor ad said, "I'm sure". lena takes out her breif case and takes the tape player and the tapes out and sets them on the table, my sponsor grabs my hand and says to me, "Frankie you will have to apply all the courage and faith you have learned so far in Recovery because this is going to make you upset" "some spots on the tapes you will hear joy and happiness but others will be a devastating reminder of what happened to you in your past", I looked at her she seen the fear I my eyes but I insisted and wanted to hear it, I wanted to get it over with so I had answers to a lot of my choices I had made and why those choices and to figure out why I had so much anger. Then I can move on with my life and never look back at whatever it was I had on those tapes, I was ready to move on with my life.

I sat on the couch and my sponsor said "we will be in the next room so that you can do this in private and in peace" I agreed, she gave me a hug and so did lena and she hands me the 2 tapes as they walk out of the room shutting the door behind them. I put in the first tape ad hit play. The first tape consist of all I had spoke about when he would make me touch him starting from six years old until I was seventeen and he had threatened me to never tell or he would do it to my sisters, I sat there and could feel the tears roll down my cheeks, I also spoke a lot about the kids, my sisters and brothers, how I was so upset at my mom for leaving me there when she went to France and took the three youngest and left me and my other brother with him. I spoke on how my brother and I got so close that summer and stuck together like glue, how I thought that my brother might of known I was being abused because he would never leave me alone with that ugly mean man, we even stayed in each others rooms at night, he would sleep on the floor right next to my bed as if he was protecting me but I never said a word about it because I didn't know for sure if he knew or not so I kept quiet. I continued to talk about how he had let his friend Bud move his camper in our yard also and I didn't like him either, he scared me, he would look at me in a nasty way so I always made sure I kept my distence from that guy, and my brother like I said would ever leave my side so I was safe. I also spoke about how drunk my step dad would get and he had woke me and my brother up one night because we had left a pa soaking in the sink, my step dad had been out that night like every night when my mom was gone and he would get home very late but was so drunk he would pass outas soo as he got in the house and I was so happy, I also spoke about how Bud would be outside in the dark and watch me do dishes through the window so he could see me but I couldn't see him but I knew he was there, but my brother was also there helping me, he has seen Bud peeking through the windows and I had spoke about how he opens the kitchen door and tells him in a mean tone that if he even thought about touching me or anything that he was going to kill him. That's what made me realize that he had to of known of the abuse because he protected me with every step I took. I sat there tears running down my face as I listened to the continued abuse, the touching, the hitting and the awful words he called me every time he was mad at me. A part of me wanted to turn off the tape but the other part of me wanted to hear it all so I did. I spoke about my brothers and sisters how I missed them and how I wanted to run away but didn't want to leave them there to have to take my place so I stayed. My heart was tore listening to all this, I was so angry and hurt and asked myself "why me" what did I ever do to deserve this all these years" and was I so afraid of him or his threats to keep my mouth shut and never tell a soul. The tape clicked as it was done, I jumped when it stopped. Wiping the tears on my face I take out the tape and begin to add the other tape. I reach to get my glass of tea as I look up to the sky and ask God, "why did you choose a path like this for me" "what did I ever do in my past life to deserve this all these years. Then I look back down to the tape player and hit play.

This time I talk about how when we were in France I never again wanted to live in the same house that he was in because I wasn't going to let him hurt me no more, I spoke about when I was married and how I would get hit by my father in law in the face all the time, how I was treated like crap and didn't know better so I did as I was told and shut up, when my husband was at work his family treated me like crap and as soon as he would come home they were all nice to me. As confused as I was I honestly thought this was the way of life, that women get abused in any shape or form and we just do as we are told nd never talk back. I continued to listen to the tape, I was at the part where I spoke of wanting to kill myself but couldn't leave my babys behind I loved them so much so that was out of the questions, I spoke about when I met Bill and got high for the first time, how it made me feel like I was the strongest person around, how knowone will ever hurt me again, I felt like I had all the cotroll in the world, how I felt tuff, strong, fearless and ready to conqure the world so I chased that high and all those false expectations for a long time. I spoke about how I stole from my sister and it killed me, last thing I would ever want to do is hurt my sisters and brothers, then I spoke about how they all disowned me and took my kids from me when they seen I was out of control and put the drugs before my kids, family and life. I spoke about how my step dad was now sober for a lot of years and he was always trying to make it better with me, I started to understand at this time, he was trying to be the dad I needed so bad, he was trying to help me get help, he would stand by my side and I seen in his eyes how it all killed him to see I had turned out this way and a lot because of him and misfortuns but also I had reached a age where it was all about choices, I just kept making the wrong ones. And then I spoke about being abused by other people. I sat there in tears and asked myself, "God was I that dumb" "did I really have no clue all these years and just blacked it out and continued to let people abuse me" did I think this was the way of life and just kept repeating the same patern over and over all these years? What was I searching for out of life.

I turned off the tape and sat there balling and so disappointed in myself, why did I let this happen to me all these years, and why did I turn out the way I did, I would of thought because of the abuse and hardships I had been through I would of turned better, but I now knew where all my anger came from and where I made bad choices to continue to use so I didn't have to feel anything at anytime. God I wanted to just die.

My sponsor came back in the room saying "are you ok", and I didn't answer, I just sat there crying quiet tears as if someone had beaten me, she sat next to me and put her arms around me and I sobbed even more, knowing that she didn't judge me meant so much and I knew as she had told me that no matter what she loved me unconditionally ad I really needed it right now.

My mother came to mind and I was missing her so much, I was wishing it was her holding me at that time and as I kept thinking of her I knew that once again I had to keep this secret because if my mother ever found out all this it would probably kill her inside but then again it would really piss her off to where she would hurt someone for abusing her daughter for 11 years, so I had to protect her now. Her health at this time wasn't in tip top shape and I didn't want her to get sick over this or even worse. "God I hated all these secretrs" but I have to do what I have to do, it's a choice I am making in hopes that at this time it's the best choice for all parties involved.

I spent the last part of that weekend really quiet, hurt inside so bad that the thought of using sounded so good because I knew that if I was to use right now all these feelings would go away and I wouldn't feel no pain or sorrow, but then again by now I also knew that once I would come down from using the feelings would be right back ad maybe in a worse way because if all the guilt so I did what I knew best and kept myself serounded in recovery this way I knew I was safe, for now.

My sponsor was the only perso who knew about all this and we had agreed that this is how I wanted to keep it, I didn't want to share it with my group nor anyone else, I told my sponsor that this was a secret I would have to live with until I felt it was time to expose it, and I wasn't ready to expose it any time soon.

I returned back to the rehab I was at, my sponsor dropped me off and told me that she didn't care what time of the day or night it was she was available for me if I needed to talk or if I was having to hard of a time with what I had just went through this weekend. Lying I told her I was just fine and that I would call her during the week. I walked in to the rehab and people welcomed me back saying "well well what you do for the weekend?" "Tell all that happened" "did you get laid?, did you go out and do anything fun". all I did was look at them with a fake smile and said "I just spent it with my sponsor working some steps ad relaxing". a few laughed telling me "well that's boring" and again with a fake smile I agreed. Walked I my room put down my stuff and sat on my bed thinking I wanted to just leve out of there, I wanted to just run away and didn't care where I went I needed to just go, the pain of this secret was so overwhelming it was killing me. Just at that time my roommate walks in and says "there's a meeting about to start come on lets go to it together" she follows by saying "and there some really good looking guys here too at this meeting". I pretended to laugh with her so it wouldn't show on my face that I really didn't give a dam at this point who was there. Sitting through the meeting I heard a message from the speaker that hit right I my heart. I wanted to cry right there ad then but I couldn't, there was no way I was going to let anyone know I was hurting inside so bad that I wanted to leave and I wanted to use, so I got up to go outside and smoke a cigarette, I wanted to be alone, I needed to think, I needed to figure out how I was going to deal with this and move on in my life, "easier said then done". As I sat there smoking I was thinking about what the speaker had just said I that meeting, he said "One of the biggest stumbling blocks to recovery seems to be placing unrealistic expectations on others, we need not lose faith when we become rebellious, we may fear that being in touch with our feelings will trigger an overwhelming chain reaction of pain and panic, and that it will not make us better people to judge the faults of others, and that Gradually, as we become more God-centered then self-centered, our despair turns into hope". I wish that's how I could feel, to have hope, to not fear and or to let go, but my gut was killing me and all I felt was anger, I was pissed off, at myself and at him, at myself for never ever telling anyone about all this and at him for using me and hurting me like that, God I hated him right now I just hated him.

I decided to throw myself in my recovery for the next few months and tried to not think about that weekend and just keep busy with work and my program knowing that as long as I was busy it was that much less I thought about it all, and that's exactly what I did, I pushed myself to my hardest ever, I chaired meetings I worked overtime I helped others with there problems I even got registered at Bethay College to become a drug counselor so I hardly ever had any time for myself or time to even think about that weekend and that's exactly what I wanted. When I did have time I spent it manipulating the guys in my rehab or having fun making people laugh, I liked doing that, making people laugh and I did it really good, so good that without realizing it I became quite the popular gal in my rehab, everybody knew Frankie and I was loving every minute of it.

I went on through the months moved next door to the rehab in a clean and sober house that was part of the program, it was a co-ed house and it was great, there was 2 women, my roommate and myself and 4 men in this house, we all go along great and had lots of fun, we participated in the meetings next door at the rehab and we would go to outside meetings as well, on the beach, in the flats, all over and I was loving life, I had forgot that I wanted to use I had blocked out this pain from my secret "for now" and I had just graduated from the college for my counseling so I was happy, I was still working at the restaurant full time and managed to even go out with a guy or two, never wanting to commit but felt like I just needed that wanting to be wanted feeling, and it worked.

It's now July 4th 1997 and I was celebrating 2 years clean. I felt so good, I never would of thought I would of made it this far but I did, I was asked to speak that night I the meeting ad I had agreed, I was so nervous and had asked my sponsor what was I do talk about. She tells me "tell your story Frankie, talk about your experiences, strengths and hopes". I gave her the look of fear and she grabs my hand saying, "there are some things you share with just your sponsor and other things about your past you can share in group, you will know which is which". I was like ok I can do this ot a problem, I mean I seen so many people share in meeting it should be that hard and I will only tell what I want them to know and keep for myself the things I don't want to tell because I felt wasn't for them to hear.

I leave my sober house to walk next door for the meeting, I was all dressed up, had my makeup on perfect, my hair down blew with the wind, I had on my tight jeans and a white blouse that was unbuttoned right to the middle of my cleavage and my boots with 4 inch heels, and thought I was looking great. When I walked in the rehab I about died. There were so many people there, all knew it was my two year birthday and all were there for support and wanted to hear my story. People started to come towards me to hug me and congratulate me, my sponsor whispers in my ear "all these people Frankie love you because you have in one way or another made a difference in there lives so tonight there all here for you". Good lord I started to feel my hands shake as I sat down in the front row waiting to get called up to speak, I cant do this, im so nervous I wont be able to talk, and as all these feelings were going through my head, again my sponsor tells me " your going to do just fine, get up there be honest and make a difference".

Yea right make a difference, hell I wasn't about to tell them I was raped for 11 years, and what was I to tell them, how I used drugs?, God I wasn't ready for this, and I was going through my head I hear clapping and my name being called to the podium, I hear people saying "yea you go Frankie whoo hoo". I squeeze my sponsors hand and get up to walk up to the podium, I look at everyone and say, "my name is Frankie ad I'm an addict" everyone responds with "Hi Frankie", then the room gets quiet, I look at everyone and it seemed like there was about 200 people there, I take a swallow and start talking, before you know it I was telling my story on how I was before where I was when I was using and how I got here to the program, It was coming out like as if every word was a sign of relief, I stayed calm and remembered to express that if it wasn't for this program I would probably be

Dead by now or in a mental hospital or even in an alley all alone. I spoke for almost an hour, expressing every aspect of my awful life except the part about my secret. That was not going to be put out there, I wasn't ready and may never be for that but it was ok, everything else I spoke about was the truth and I was feeling so releaved like pain was being escorted out of my heart and soul. I would glance at my sponsor from time to time as I spoke and the look on her face was as if she was so proud of me, it made me feel so good. I end my speech by saying "there's no person, place or thing worth your life today." people stood up and clapped there hands I was like in a daze from this feeling I had in my heart, something was lifted because I felt so much more at peace, and I was enjoying this good feeling I had inside.

When the meeting was over I was overwhelmed by everyone coming up to me saying how they loved my story, how I had a lot to say that gave them hope and faith, they were hugging me and making me feel like I really did make a difference in some of them and it felt so good, I felt like I was finally giving back to people what was given to me in this program. Now move on people I need a smoke as I laughed and joked but walked my way out side to have that smoke.

Five years in recovery now, I'm working for drug court doing some advocate work with first time drug offender's, working for the same judge who gave me this opportunity to make a difference In my life, I have my son back the youngest Aaron, I have a nice house near the beach, and I have 4 clean and sober houses working on getting another one. I'm in touch with my two other children, Angelique and Christophe also and things are good. I'm sitting I my office at home, coffee in my hand it's 7 am and I'm looking around me thinking how grateful I am to have come this far. I am surrounded by wonderful people in my life all from recovery and have made a good decent name for myself here in Santa Cruz. I'm happy, really happy.

I'm not in a relationship but have plenty of men in my life that wouldn't mind hooking up for a few hours in the mid of night. Not that I can just pick and choose but if I'm in the mood I know where to go. I'm feeling great and so content. I am in touch with my family again and things are going good with them ad me. Yes I do think about my secret but have decided that it's to just keep it to myself for now. I remember that during my addiction I did things that were not very nice at all and I wasn't proud of myself for it, which brought me to the secret because he ws an alcoholic at the time and a real bad one, but now he had years sober and was a totally different man. This doesn't mean I have forgiven him for what he did, it just meas that sometimes the past is best left in the past. I know that every time I spend time with my family who live in Oregon I see how he is totally different and truly acts like a Father to me, he gives me words of advice and he shows me that he really loves me, like a Father should live his daughter, I'm sure he knows that I know but we never talk about it and his actions show me he is truly living day to day praying that I forgive him, I'm sure it tortures him every time he see's me and deep inside I hope it does because it's something I never want him to forget, it's his own little punishment of hell and I cant help him nor want to, I want him to feel like crap every time he thinks about what he did, it's better then going to jail or loseing his family. I do have to say that today I truly love him as my Father, he stands by me when others want to drama about my past in the family, he treats me good and with respect when I'm around him and we have even become very close as a Father and daughter should be. I wish I had this kind of relationship with him when I was younger but least I have it now so im content with the challenges God has put in front of me and my choices on how I have dealt with them.

I love my family in Oregon so much, I have my favorites with my brothers and sisters which is commin and I love my mother with all my heart, she will never know how much I love her and that's ok, I can only say it so many times and show it to her to my best, but I simply adore her, she is the strongest woman I have ever known, I have seen her go through so much in life as I was growing up and to see how she is today is simply amazing. She is still so beautiful and takes very good care of herself that people think she is on her fiftys when she is in her seventies. Now that's what I call a damn good woman. I look up to her, look forward to seeing her so much every time I go to Oregon, and she has no clue how much I adore her, yes she knows I love her but the depth of it she has no idea and that's ok, I alone know things that knowone else knows about her and just to know and see how she has turned out is breath taking and heart warming. My step dad and I have formed a real good father daughter relationship that I hang on to it with every inch of hope that it always stays that way, I can dwell on the past all I want, what's important is that I have it now and even though I carry my secret with me or wish I had this relationship with him when I was younger, I simply hold o to the moment and try not to ruion it with my thought of the past, as long as I stay strong, show that im a better person today and keep my head up continuing to do as good as I am and making a difference in others live's then I'm happy, content and free of any fear or secret.

My son Aaron and I have formed a strong relationship, we go out to eat together, we go to the movies and have fun just spending time with each other. If only he could stay young forever because I know the day will come where he wont want to spend time with mom like we do now so I'm going to take advantage of it every moment I can.

A lot of the people I go to meetings with and work with have Bike's mostly Harleys and I was getting tired of riding on the back of someone's bike every time we went for rides which were almost every weekend and during the week, so I decided to get me my own Harley.

What a feeling that was to have my first very own Harley, wow the feeling was so overwhelming I couldn't speak when I sat on my bike for the first time. This was mine it was really mine, I had worked so hard for this and earned every bit of it, I was so proud and looked up to the sky thinking of Tony kowig he was watching me from heave and was happy for me. I missed him so much, and now that I had my own bike I missed him even more. I went to the 8 pm meeting on my bike wanting to show it off, it was a sportster 1999 and only had 800 miles on it, it was black with pin stripes and the nme Harley Davidson on the tank, the tank was changed from a small one to a wide tank ad the crome shined like fireworks in the sky at night, I was in love, with my bike, it made me happy, feel proud and felt like everyone was so excited for me, how grateful I felt.

My son wasn't sure about me having a bike, I think he was afraid that I would get hurt, but I would always reasure him that I would be just fine. He liked it and always showed it off to his friends when they were at the house, I could her him from the kitchen when he was in the garage with his friends and would show them my harley I would chuckel because the tone of his voice was like he was happy and excited that we had a Harley in our garage.

It was summer and I would go to so may meetings just so I could ride my bike and of course show it off and the weekends the guys from San Jose would come down to the breakfast meeting, then we would all go to half moon bay to have lunch which was about a 45 miute ride from Santa Cruz, and every weekend it seemed the group got bigger and bigger, I remember on weekend there were about 60 of us that went to lunch then we would ride along the ocean on hwy 101, it was beautiful and so spiritual for me, feeling that wind in my face made me forget I ever ever had any problems in life and felt free as a bird flying in the air, God I loved it so much, I had finally found my serenity and sense of freedom from any people, places or things that made me sad or indifferent. And the company I was with were men and women in the program that I knew truly cared and loved me unconditionally, what else could I ask for, I had it made, my own business, my family back In my life, my kids back, my recovery going strong, my friends, my God that really cared and the feeling of happiness and love in my heart. I wasn't about to do anything to lose any of this, I had earned it the hard way but it was mine and for the first time in my whole life I knew this is what I wanted, I wasn't about to lose any of this or the way I felt so I continued to work hard in all areas of my life.

I am now 45 years old and my life is still going great, my recovery is very strong, I'm involved in all areas of recovery to help make a difference in other peoples lives, I was still single and liked it that way, I had a few relationships but they didn't last long, my freedom meant more to me at the time that being tied down wasn't something I wanted. When I wanted some romance in my life I knew where to go, it wasn't nice of me to maybe use these guys for my advantage but I wasn't ashamed of it either. My son was growing up to fast and we weren't as close as we were when he was smaller but we still kept that bond, I was close with my other 2 children and with a step daughter Kristy whom I took in when she was younger and we were very close. She knew me when I was using and supported me I my recovery, I loved her very much, it was like in her eyes I could do no wrong, that's how she worshiped me and I loved her for that. My business was going really well and my life was just so good. I would go to Oregon on vacation to visit family and they came to me to visit so that was great also. I was also addicted to the internet playing Gammon on line with other folks and meeting great people, a few of them had come to meet me that had known me at least a year or more while we all played gammon on line and I had yet again made more friends. From New York a great couple that I consider today as family, from Arkansas a couple there also that was like family they were great, and other states that I met great people. I had a best friend Tanya who would always tease me about how Frakie knew no strangers. She was so awesome and still is, she was what we call in recovery a normie, someone who never did drugs but because of our friendship she supported my recovery and went with me to meetings all the time, we would sit not to close to the front but not to close to the back, right where we could see almost everyone and we were on a roll taking everyones inventory and laughing among ourselves when we would see someone making fools of them selves, she was simply awesome to be around and the bestest friend I had ever had, it was really nice.

I was talking to the judge from drug court after work one day and he tells me that there was a lot of help needed in recovery at the drug court in Arkansas, that they had just started it up and needed people like me to help them, he had told me that it would be a opportunity of a lifetime. Well I was talking to some friends I knew in Arkansas and I went home that night thinking it over really hard. "did I really want to make such a drastic change" and "was it really going to be the opportunity of my life" I had never been to Arkansas but "I'm sure it wasn't that much different from California" so I decided to go to Arkansas for a week just to check it out, I had made arrangements with my friends from Arkasas to stay with them and I would see how it was down there. My son was like "Arkansas? Your kidding right" well I didn't tell him nothing because I knew it was going to be a fight so I just told him I was going to visit friends for a week, he would be staying with a friend of ours Gary who was like a Father to Aaron and my son loved him so I knew he would be safe while I was gone, so I packed my bags and off I go to Arkansas.

Things were really different in Arkansas, the kids there were much more well behaved then in California. They would say yes ma'am or yes sir to any grown up that addressed them, and I liked the way people had respect for others, it was more what I would call homely. I checked in for the schools for my son which I liked a lot they were less filled and I felt gave the child more one o one with the teacher, I looked at the possibility for my work and really believed that it was a go for me. The people I was staying with Roni and Eddie were absolutely wonderful, I had met them on line five years prior to then playing Gammon and we got very close, they treated me like I was a part of the family and the feeling was safe and loved more then I could of ever ask for. They had fun with me thinking I had a accent from California when I turn I thought they were the ones with the accent and they got a kick out of teaseing me about dear in july and telling me I was going to go snipe hunting. At first I thought it was for real but found out different and it was all in fun. I had also met a guy there who was a friend of Roni and Eddie and we met, he seemed very nice and very well polite towards women, his name was David. He lead me to believe that he wanted to keep in touch with me when I returned to Califoria ad I agreed. After having a great wonderful time in Arkansas it was time for me to return to California and it was hard saying goodbye to my friends who had taken me in as if I was one of theres, they were so wonderful and hoped that one day I could return the faver.

I flew back to California and it was good being home seeing my son and my friends, I was well known in Santa Cruz, for my work and my recovery everyone knew Frankie, I was me as I am, didn't have to put on a show or try to be someone I wasn't it was clear I was me for me and nothing else and this made me happy, I lived near the beach in a 2600 sq home that was very nice and my son had everything he needed and then some. Yes I spoiled him because I felt bad doing to him what I did when I was using and put my drugs before him so I felt I had somew making up to do so whatever he wanted he basicly got. But he was at that age where he was starting to sneak out at ight and stealing money from me, his grades were going down fast and I was getting really worried, when I had found out he got kicked off the football team because of his grades is when I really started to worry and knew I had to do something or I was going to lose him to the system for doing bad things, he had good friends but he also had a few that didn't care about nothing but having fun and drinking and getting high. That thought killed me and I knew I had to do something before I lost my boy to jail or God knows what. He was getting in fights and coming home at times really bad and it killed me. I thought for a long time then decided that we were going to move to Arkansas, I figured I would sell my business to my assistant and I could pick up my work for drug court there in Arkansas it was in the works of getting started there so I would be fresh meat sort of speak to start work there, I had spoke to a guy from there who had promised me a spot so I wasn't worried. I got a U-Haul and packed up all the things I could ad what I didt I would sell. I had my Harley and figured I should probably sell it as well because I didn't recall seeing anyone on Harleys when I was in Arkansas so why not, I called my fried Roni in Arkansas and asked her to help me find a home and help me drive from California to Arkansas, and without even thinking twice she had answered yes.

I will never forget the night we left Santa Cruz, I started to think to myself oh my God what was I doing, my son was crying it killed me in my heart, but it was to late now all was packed and off we were for the road trip. It took us 3 days to get to Texarkana Arkansas from California, we drove none stop, we just stoped for food and gas that was it. We arrive to Texarkana and as we drove up to Roni's and Eddie's house I thought to myself this is going to be scary to yet start all over again but it wasn't the first time for me and I wasn't afraid to do it so I took a deep breath and looked at my son and my dog and thought ok here we are kiddos, I looked around me and stepped out of the car ready to start my new life in Fouke Arkansas.

We stayed at Roni's house for about 2 months until we finally found a house to put on there property, I had to fix it up and it took all the money I had on me almost, I had found a job because the guy from drug court didn't work out he had got laid off before he even got on so I was given false hope to having a job. I thought to myself lord what have I done, but kept it to myself and did what I had to do. I worked all the time my son went to school and was doing much better then he was in California so least this made me happy, he kept telling me how he hated it there and why did we ever move, I would ask myself the same thing at times but it was a done deal so instead of mopeing on the same thought I know I had to give it the best I had which I did. I would also see David a lot until I found out he had a girlfriend and was going to get married but he neglected to tell me that, I wasn't shocked because I knew I had been used and I had to keep it together for myself and my son, it was bad enough we were in the middle of knowheres and I had no time to feel sorry for a choice I had made so I did what I do best and that was to make the best out of what we had. I didn't go to meetings for a good 3 years because I had gone to one and I didn't like it so I just didn't go, I stayed clean because with working so much and keeping my son focused in sports. I had a full plate and didn't even think about using or nothing like that, which was good. I started to meet new friends from where I worked and met the police and sheriff department because they would come to my work a lot to eat and get gas so it was good for me knowing I was always safe. I had met a few cops that I had gone out with and as always got my heart broke but nothing I wasn't used too. I was the queen of getting my heart broke so I didn't get to close to many people because of it, I focused on my work and my son. It was so hard living in Arkansas because I was yet again struggling, I had a half ass job that didn't pay much but we made it through every month, I was living in a trailor and out in the middle of know wheres, I remember sitting out side one night late after work and asking myself, "what have I done" I was thinking bout all I had in California with my successful business, money in the bank a Harley a good car and could do almost anything I wanted, my son lacked of nothing and I was able to shop or give him basically whatever he wanted and now look at me here in the middle of know where's struggling and didn't have a pot to piss in, and surrounded by bugs I had never seen before in my life out here, lighting bugs, sticks with legs and the list goes on. All the expectations I had coming here for it to be shaddered and being at a point where I had nothing but the basics. I was smarter then this, to just go by false promises I had made to myself, I missed California the beach my friends and especially my income and having money in the bank to do as I wished. I was sitting looking around me and realized I had made a huge mistake by letting everything go in California and being here with nothing. As I looked around there were nothing but woods all around me and I was about 45 minutes from town, the only neighbor I had was my wonderful friends Roni and Eddie who lived next door about 500 ft from me and I was on there land. All I had was this single wide trailer, my furniture, my car and my son, that was it!! Good God what have I done I said to myself again and I started to cry, my son was asleep in his room so I was safe that know one would see me. All the money I had in California I had used to pay for this and that for the move the plane ticket for one of the drivers that helped bring me here and once I got here all I had was about ten thousand dollars to my name so I was broke. I felt like I had once again lost everything and fallen to hit yet another bottom but this time I did it clean from drugs. And I had my friends Roni and Eddie who always gave me hope, especially Roni because she understood, she knew how I felt and she would keep me going so that I would stay out of this self pity I was in, she always gave me words of encouragement and she just knew, I didn't have to sit there and tell her how bad I felt she just knew and always did everything she could to keep me focused on Today and to move forward, if I didn't have her during this move and these months I was on a down spell I would of never made it, she means more to me then she will ever know, and I hope one day to show her and I mean really show her how special she is to my life.

I continued to work hard, I finally got myself a better car and had moved from the trailor to a house closer to town so things were starting to look up for me, I spent time at my sons games and tried to participate in all his affares while he was still in high school, he was doing really good, he was chageing doing good in school and finally seemed to be a little more happy, and to be honest that's all I ever wanted was to see him make it and be happy. I would go out here and there with friends and at times with a male friend but none of them seemed to capture my heart I a way that I wanted to spend the rest of my life with them, maybe it was because I was hurt so many times I had given up on that thought, then I met Tom, he was a cowboy, old school type guy, very nice, polite and so thoughtful I liked him right away, we became friends and seemed to have so much fun every time we were together that I always looked forward to seeing him, my friends all liked him ad especially my friend Roni, if she said she liked him then you knew he must be a good guy because she would tell me about how guys were all jerks or if I dated one she made sure to let me know how she felt bout him and even tell the guy, "if you hurt my friend you will deal with me" I loved her she was always looking out for me and I felt special, she was like my sister and I simply adored her as my friend. Her husband Eddie was the same way he treated me like family so with them in my life I never felt alone and it was really nice knowing there were still some great people out here in this world. Tom and I continued to date and the more we saw each other the more serious we got, he was so easy to love, he was simple and never asked for nothing but to spend time with me, my son also really liked him which made it even that much better and so did Eddie and Roni, they were smart people and knew a good man when they seen one so life was starting to look much brighter for me, my son had good friends and finally graduated from high school, I was so proud of that and that's when tom asked me to marry him. To be honest I wasn't even expecting it and he caught me by surprise but I loved him so much by that time that I didn't hesitate and said yes right away, he put a diamond ring on my finger that was so beautiful I had never seen one so pretty and I wore it with pride, we were going to Oregon for a week for my parents to meet him and as I expected they all loved him to death, there was nothing about him not to love he was perfect. He had a great job he had been at for 18 years, he had his own home and land, he had his feet solid on the ground and knew what he wated out of life, that's a lot more then I could say about the ones I had dated in the years before.

So tom and I move in together and plan our wedding. I was so excited because I was going to have my whole family there and that meant more to me then anything. It was so cold the day of the wedding I was disappointed hoping that everyone could come, it ws freezing outside and I knew some people wouldn't be able to make it like toms mom she lived to far away to travel this far in that kind of waether so I made sure to keep things from our wedding to give to her. All my family was there except one of my sisters but that was ok I was happy that they did there best to be there for my special day. I was so happy, I ws going to be married to the mn of my dreams, he was perfect for me and I for him we just matched so well together and I had lots of friends and family there to support this special day. I was working for Orr Cheverolet at the time so I had friends from there that came, family nd friends I had made here through out the years so I was very happy. My youngest son and my daughter nd her daughter was there my oldest son lived in France and couldn't be there but I knew his heart was there for me and that meant a lot to me. Everything went well for my wedding nd I ws now married. Wow I never thought I would of ever married again, but I did and I was very happy.

A few years go by and im doing great, I go to N/A meetings regularly and make lots of great friends, I get myself a sponsor here because the one I had in California was pushing me to get one here so I did, things are going well, I had my good days and my bad days, things were changing and I would wonder what my goal in life was here in Arkansas. I had a great home went through great jobs and made a good name for myself, just like In California I was well known and people liked me for who I was not what I had. But I still felt that something was missing in my life, I wanted to make a difference in peoples lives but not enable them so what was I to do that would make an impact that would rejoice my heart. I had decided to continue to have clean and sober houses like I did in California and did so well, I started to run meetings to help out I was going to the jails to do meetings and to the womens center also, just seeing there faces and knowing I was making a difference in there lives completed me. I knew why god had sent me here, he wanted me to do what I do best, that was making a difference in peoples lives and nothing more made me feel good inside and made me feel like I was accomplishing something good that God would approve of.

I am now 54 years old, married to the same man whom is a wonderful husband, my children are all near me so I see them on a regular basis, I talk to my family every week sometimes more, I have a relationship with my Mother today I wouldn't trade for the world, she is my rock and my life I simply love and adore her with all my heart. I have a wonderful sponsor here and friends that are incredible I have found a spot in my heart I can finally call peace. I have written letters to my mother and my step dad to let them know I love them and I forgive him or her for whatever happened in the past that I had worked through it and I was ok today, I have a God in my life that is simply wonderful and loves me unconditionally, I continue to tell my story any time im asked to speak in hopes that if anyone out there has gone through what I have or is going through it I want them to know it will all be ok. I have realized that its not fair nor right that I had to go through what I did to become who I am today, but I also feel that all I have been through has made me who I am today and allows me to make choices today that I know are the right ones. My sponsor always tells me that as long as you do things with out hurting anyone and know that you have satisfied your heart by helping someone then you have done something good. I believe her because every time I give words of wisdom or help someone out how ever I do it I feel better knowing I was there for just that moment remembering I never had that as a child or beginning adulthood. So today I carry happiness in my heart, I help people without bragging bout it to others, I give from my heart the best I can knowing it isn't going to effect my marriage or family because there to important to me today. I can finally rest in peace knowing I have made all my amends to those I have hurt in one way or another, I have found my soul mate, my husband and I have my family back I my life. Nothing makes me happier. No matter what the past has done to me, today I am stronger because of it; I am solid on my feet and not afraid to attack anything that is put before me. People come into your life for a reason, a season or a lifetime.

When you know which one it is, you will know what to do for that person.

When someone is in your life for a REASON, it is usually to meet a need you have expressed. They have come to assist you through a difficulty,

To provide you with guidance and support, to aid you physically, emotionally or spiritually. They may seem like a godsend and they are.

They are there for the reason you need them to be.

Then, without any wrongdoing on your part or at an inconvenient time,

This person will say or do something to bring the relationship to an end.

Sometimes they die. Sometimes they walk away. Sometimes they act up and force you to take a stand. What we must realize is that our need has been met, our desire fulfilled, their work is done. The prayer you sent up has been answered and now it is time to move on. Some people come into your life for a SEASON, because your turn has come to share, grow or learn.

They bring you an experience of peace or make you laugh. They may teach you something you have never done. They usually give you an unbelievable amount of joy.

Believe it, it is real. But only for a season. LIFETIME relationships teach you lifetime lessons, Things you must build upon in order to have a solid emotional foundation. Your job is to accept the lesson, Love the person and put what you have learned to use in all other relationships and areas of your life It is said that love is blind but friendship is clairvoyant

Thank you for being a part of my life, whether you were a reason, a season or a lifetime.

Stand Up!!... For what you believe in. Stand for something or you will fall for anything... "Let us not be weary in doing good; for at the proper time, we will reap a harvest if we do not give up. Therefore, as we have opportunity, let us do good..." Reach Up!!... For something higher. "Trust in the Lord with all your heart, and lean not unto your own understanding. In all your ways, acknowledge Him, and He will direct your path." Dress Up!! The best way to dress up is to put on a smile. A smile is an inexpensive way to improve your looks. Decide to have a good day. Enjoy today to the fullest, because tomorrow is not promised.

So today I treat it like it's the first day of the rest of my life. Today I do not worry about anything; instead I PRAY ABOUT EVERYTHING." Because I really feel I have been giving a second chance at life, yes I have worked hard to get where I am today but because I have faith in my heart today and believe that God is really guiding me through the path of hopefulness then I believe I have a great chance in having more great wonderful years ahead of me to be who and what I am today. I am grateful to my readers, my family my friends and my God for being there for me today unconditionally and understanding me for who and what I am, what I need and want today. Thanks to N/A in my life and having a heart filled with peace and happiness today is a feeling I will cherish forever. I was just told the other day " isn't it a little late in life to feel like you do now", my answer was to them, " it's never to late to be happy and have forgiveness in my heart like I do today so NO it's never to late. I wish knowone have to go through my life as I did, but if I can give words of wisdom and help from my experiences someone from having to go through what I did then I will be there for them.

The reason I wrote this book was for my own self peace and in hopes to help a lot of people out there going through hard times ad wondering "why me". I'm hoping from my experiences, strengths and hopes that I give courage to you knowing that if you allow it and make the right choices in your life that everything cn change and be turned around to where your life can and will be so much better. My story applies a lot to people in recovery but also anyone out there who simply needs that word of encouragement. If I can offer simply that to you then I have done something good.

I know that for the rest of my life there will be people who will throw my past in my face, my drug using my being out there doing bad things and all the lieing, cheating and stealing I did, but it's ok with me because Today I owe knowone nothing but to offer them who I am and who I have become. I will not allow anyone to have the power today to try to control me or manipulate me in hurting my feelings, if they succeed in doing so that's because I have allowed it because today I have choices and only I can make that final choice of how my life goes and what I do about it. I am far from perfect and I will still make mistakes but I believe that as long as I learn from them and don't repeat them then

I will be just fine. I have forgiven all those who have hurt or used me in the past and I am hoping that the ones I have hurt and done wrong forgive me as well. If they haven't done so then there is nothing I can do about that because today im "ME" a good woman a good mother a good daughter a good sister and friend and a normal human being that is doing the best that I can to get by everyday clean from drugs and having a normal life. I have 14 years clean as of july 4th 2009 and I am proud of all the hard work I have put into my recovery to be who I am today, I do have to thank N/A, my sponsor's my family and friends who have supported me through my journey and believed in me knowing I did the right thing and that I have become who I should of always been sense the very beginning, "me".

Once I was entirely ready to have my character defects removed, I was entirely ready! Ironically that's when my troubles started, the more I struggled to rid myself of a particular defect, the stronger that shortcoming seemed to become. It is truly humbling to realize that not only am I powerless over my addiction, people places and things but even my own defects of character. This journey I have overcome through out my life never suggested that I rid myself of my shortcomings, but that I ask my higher power to rid me of them. I would plead with my higher power to do for me what I couldn't do for myself. I realized that my way of thinking was dominated by fear and I needed to do something about it. I found willingness to change my old ways of thinking and things I did, so I traded in my old cynical doubts for new affirmations of hope and realized it was so well worth the risk. As you see through my journey I found a way of life to live life on lifes terms and to make a difference in peoples lives. Today I live my life one day at a time, with out fear and great pride that no matter what comes my way I can handle it to my best ability, I will give as much as I can from my heart and soul to make someone smile and make my day, I will make choices that are from knowone but myself giving me the final say to what I need to do or not do. I walk with my feet solid on the ground, head held up high and a sense of knowledge that only I know my capabilities. I will do all I can to make a difference on peoples lives but not restrict myself from those I love the most. I am humble today, I'm very happy within and very content that I was given another chance at life to live it the way I want to live it and know that the path I take today is the right one filled with good people, places and things with people who love me unconditionally. I may now be 54 years old but its never to late to live life to its fullest and that's exactly what I'm doing. I will never forget what Tony said to me before he died.

"Being true to yourself takes guts, first, you've got to face everything around you and figure out what is important; what you think really counts. Second, you've got to interact with a lot of people who may see things differently. But life has lots of smiles and frowns, as days have there ups and downs. And if you are true to yourself in all that you do, and if you keep working to make your dreams come true, then you will achieve success just by doing your best. You've got everything it takes to be true to you."

My goal for writing this book was to be able to make a difference in others lives, I have given speeches in many different places and states, as I stand there and tell others to hold no secrets and rid yourself of any past hurts so you can go on and live a functional life but I inside kept my own secrets and I felt like a hypocrite every time I would walk out a door from giving a speech, so I decided that I had to apply to myself what I was preaching and once I did I finally felt hole. My book is not out to hurt any one it's a self help book to help those who are going through what I did and learn what to do to better there lives, if I can do it any one can do it.

I'm sitting outside with a cup of coffee in my hands feeling the sun on my face, watching my grandchildren play together, my children are gathered around talking up a storm and laughing, my husband cooking steaks on the grill and for some reason I'm so sad all of the sudden I'm real sad inside. I have all the sudden realized that my marriage is over …something is wrong and I haven't yet figured out what but trust me I will investigate and handle this task as well with my head up strong and my heart protected. Nothing I'm not used too but something I will take care of… (to be continued)

My journey may have been tuff at times but it has made me who I am today and to feel what I feel at this moment I wouldn't trade in for anything. Do I forgive all the people, places and things that have hurt me in the past ABSOLUTELY , do people forgive me for all the harm

I have caused along the way. I SURELY HOPE SO WITH ALL MY HEART. I will get my past thrown in my face from time to time for the rest of my life but I'm ok with it because today I owe know one any kind of explanation and I have made all my amends and I have done what I have done it's in the past so that's where I leave it. Some will enjoy reminding me just because they feel good wanting to try to make me feel bad, but today I do not give any person, place or thing that kind of power over me and I'm proud of that, I can walk with my head high and not have to look over my shoulder. I'm a great mother, a wonderful friend, a good daughter and sister and I love myself for who I am and all my strength.

Thank you God and to all of you who believed in me, I couldn't of done this without you. God bless you all.

FRANKIE MARIE

May God bless you...Frankie

About The Author

Frankie Marie is a woman of many tasks. She specializes in wanting to make a difference in peoples lives that has to do with chemical dependence, or any addict, troubled or dysfunctional families or simply sharing her story in hopes that someone will hear something that will help them change there lives. Her first book was to simply get you acquainted with her and her ways, in the books to come she will share a lot if her experiences, strengths and hopes with you knowing that someone out there can relate and need to hear what she has to say so they can make changes in there lives and know its going to be ok...

Frankie is a woman that tends to know no strangers, she likes to laugh and have fun on a daily basis and lives life one day at a time...

Frankie will share with you some painful times, people she has hurt and how she made it through it all to become who she is today, she loves her readers and is always willing to read there e-mails to hear what they have to say about her book, if you wish to e-mail her contact is FrankiesGratitudeSpeaks@hotmail.com